Baedeker's
BRUSSELS

Imprint

Cover picture: The Grand'Place

84 colour photographs
19 maps and plans, 1 large city map

Conception and editorial work:
Redaktionsbüro Harenberg, Schwerte
English language: Alec Court

Cartography:
George Schiffner, Lahr
Gert Oberländer, Munich
Hallwag AG, Berne (city map)

Text: Hans von Stahlborn, Brussels
Continuation: Helmut Linde, Reutlingen
Consultant: Sissi Puttaert, Brussels

General direction:
Dr Peter Baumgarten, Baedeker Stuttgart

English translation:
Babel Translations, Norwich

Source of illustrations:
CGT Belgien (3), Esterhazy (4), Fototeca EG (1), Historia-Photo (4), Messerschmidt (4),
Rogge (8), Sperber (55), Suddeutscher Verlage (3), Verkehrsbetriebe Brüssel (1), ZEFA (1)

Following the tradition established by Karl Baedeker in 1844, sights of particular interest and hotels or restaurants of particular quality are distinguished by either one or two asterisks.

To make it easier to locate the various sights listed in the "A to Z" section of the Guide, their coordinates on the large city plan are shown in red at the head of each entry.

Only a selection of hotels, restaurants and shops can be given: no reflection is implied, therefore, on establishments not included.

In a time of rapid change it is difficult to ensure that all the information given is entirely accurate and up to date, and the possibility of error can never be entirely eliminated. Although the publishers can accept no responsibility for inaccuracies and omissions, they are always grateful for corrections and suggestions for improvement.

Licensed user:
Mairs Geographischer Verlag GmbH & Co., Ostfildern-Kemnat bei Stuttgart

Reproductions:
Gölz Repro-Service GmbH, Ludwigsburg

The name *Baedeker* is a registered trademark

Printed in Great Britain by Jarrold & Sons Ltd, Norwich

0–13–368788–0

Contents

Preface

This Pocket Guide to Brussels is one of the new generation of Baedeker city guides.

Baedeker pocket guides, illustrated throughout in colour, are designed to meet the needs of the modern traveller. They are quick and easy to consult, with the principal sights described in alphabetical order and practical details about opening times, how to get there, etc., shown in the margin.

Each guide is divided into three parts. The first part gives a general account of the city, its history, notable personalities and so on; in the second part the principal sights are described; and the third part contains a variety of practical information designed to help visitors to find their way about and make the most of their stay.

The new guides are abundantly illustrated and contain numbers of newly drawn plans. At the back of the book is a large city map, and each entry in the main part of the guide gives the coordinates of the square on the map in which the particular feature can be located. Users of this guide, therefore, will have no difficulty in finding what they want to see.

Facts and Figures

Coat of arms
of Brussels,
capital of Belgium

General

Brussels ("Bruxelles" in French, "Brussel" in Flemish), capital of the Province of Brabant, is also the capital of the Kingdom of Belgium. Here is the King's official residence and the seat of the Government and the Parliament. Belgium is a constitutional Parliamentary monarchy with a Constitution dating from 1831.

Capital

Situated on about latitude 50°50'N and longitude 4°20'E, its height above sea-level ranges from 15 m (46 ft) in the central boulevards area to 52 m (170 ft) in the Place Madou and 100 m (328 ft) between the Parc du Forêt and the Parc Duden. The city owes its topography to the River Senne which traverses it from south-west to north-east. The Willebroeck Canal runs roughly parallel with the Senne and over the years a great many industrial firms have been established along its course.

Situation

The international dialling code for Belgium is 32 and the area code for Brussels is 2.

Dialling code

Greater Brussels, consisting of the city centre and 18 suburban communes, has a population of 990,000, about 240,000 of whom are foreigners. In all the city covers an area of 16,179 ha (40,440 acres).

Area and population

Officially Brussels is bilingual, as are its suburbs, but the city centre forms a predominantly French-speaking island close to the southern border of the Flemish (Dutch) linguistic territory. Many of those living in the city, particularly in the working-class areas, speak Brussels dialects in which French and Dutch intermingle.

Language

Greater Brussels consists of 19 largely independent communes. Besides the Commune de Bruxelles, which includes the city centre, a narrow strip of the Upper Town and the area around the Palace of Laeken and the Royal Palace, there are the communes of Uccle, Anderlecht, Watermael-Boitsfort, Auderghem, Woluwe-St-Lambert, Woluwe-St-Pierre, Forest, Ixelles, Molenbeek, St-Jean, Evere, Jette, Etterbeek, Berchem Ste-Agathe, St-Gilles, Ganshoren, Koekelberg, and St-Josse-ten-Noode. All the communes have their own Mayor (Bourgmestre) and a Communal Council (Conseil communal). Representatives of the 19 communes sit on the Greater Brusels Council (Conseil d'Agglomération), which mainly has a co-ordinating function. The Chairman of the Conseil d'Agglomération has to stand for election every 4 years and is a Mayor from one of the 19 communes. The situation is somewhat confused at the moment since Brussels, which up until now has been treated separately, is also due to become a region on its own as part of Belgian regional reform. All

Administration

◀ *The Grand'Place with its Guildhalls – Brussels' "front room"*

9

attempts at a settlement so far have foundered on the language problems and the question of possibly extending the Brussels region beyond the boundaries of the present metropolitan area.

International institutions
(EEC, NATO)

Brussels is the seat of the European Communities (EEC), the NATO Council and General Secretariat and numerous other public and private international organisations and institutions. The city has an unusually large diplomatic presence since many States have diplomats accredited to the EEC and NATO as well as to the King of the Belgians.

Population and Religion

Population

Belgium lies on the frontier between the Germanic and the Romance linguistic areas. This applies particularly strongly to Brussels which represents a predominantly French-speaking (Walloon) enclave in Flemish (i.e. Dutch-speaking) territory. This also carries over into the city where one comes across people of totally opposing types and temperaments – elegant women clearly modelling themselves on Parisian fashion-plates alongside plodding, rather rustic folk who could have stepped straight out of a Bruegel painting, and bustling businessmen, with a Germanic air about them, next to Gallic ladies' men that one would have expected to see on the Champs-Elysées rather than in the heart of Brabant.

All Bruxellois share an unusual openness and directness, as well as an almost boundless tolerance towards those of a different persuasion. The so-called language problem has never really played much of a role in Brussels daily life. Latterly it has been the politicians who for some years, for different political – and economic – interests, have deliberately been bringing this problem forward. Nowadays many Bruxellois switch unthinkingly from one language to the other, often mixing Dutch and French words together in the same sentence, or lapsing into their Brussels dialects.

Because of the many international institutions in Brussels it has become more cosmopolitan than any other European city. Almost every fourth resident of the Belgian capital is a foreigner.

All the countries belonging to one of the international institutions based in Brussels have their own quite substantial colonies and usually their own schools and churches.

Spain provides a traditionally strong group of "guest-workers", many of whom live in the Marolles quarter. The city street scene derives an additional exotic touch from the many black and coloured people from the former Belgian colonies of the Congo and Ruanda Urundi.

In addition there is a constant stream of tourists almost throughout the year, thronging the squares and streets of the inner city, particularly around the Grand'Place, the Opéra and the central boulevards.

Religion

Most of the inhabitants of Brussels are Roman Catholic, and the city is the seat of an Archbishop, but Protestants and Jews also form substantial religious minorities.

People in Brussels

Transport

Brussels Airport (Zaventem) is located 14 km (9 miles) from the city centre. It has direct flights to most European capitals and to many destinations overseas and in the Near, Middle and Far East. It is the home base for SABENA, the Belgian airline, and in 1982 recorded over 5·2 million passengers and handled about 160,000 tons of freight.

Airport

Brussels is a centre for international, national and regional rail transport, and has direct rail links with all the major European capitals.

Railway

Transport

The Brussels expressway – the inner ring road

Canal port	Brussels canal port facilities are located in the north of the city. These were created between 1895 and 1922 by the widening of the Willebroeck Canal, constructed in the 16th c, which connects Brussels with the Rupel and thence the Scheldt. They are accessible to medium-sized vessels.
Local transport	Local transport is by bus, underground and tram. The underground network is being intensively extended. In 1985, although still incomplete, it had a total length of 42 km (26 miles).
Motorways	Belgium has had a very dense and well-lit motorway network for some years. Use of the motorways is still free of charge. Brussels is located at the hub of the Belgian motorway network which connects it with all points of the compass. The ring road speeds up through-traffic and access to the capital.

Culture

General	Brussels is Belgium's major centre for the arts and the sciences, with its University, Polytechnic, Royal Academy and many other schools of arts and crafts, and cultural institutions. Some of the city's nearly 70 museums are world-famous, such as the Musées Royaux des Beaux-Arts (see Practical Information – Museums, for a list of the major museums). The city is the headquarters for both of Belgium's State broadcasting corporations (RTBF, BRT). A number of major

Brussels Free University – one of Belgium's leading colleges

newspapers ("Le Soir", "La Libre Belgique", "Het laatste Nieuws") are published in Brussels, and various publishing companies have their base or a subsidiary here.

The Brussels Free University (Université Libre de Bruxelles), founded in 1834, is the city's leading academic institution. It has some 50,000 students and most faculties have French-speaking and Dutch-speaking departments.
A large outpost of the University of Louvain's medical faculty (Louvain-en-Woluwe) is situated in the suburb of Woluwe-St-Lambert.
Brussels is also the seat of the venerable Académie Royale des Sciences, des Lettres et des Beaux-Arts de Belgique, of the Ecole Nationale Supérieure d'Architecture et des Arts Visuels, of the Conservatoire Royal de Musique, and many other prominent academies, schools and scientific associations.

Colleges, Academies

Almost 100 cinemas and more than 30 theatres offer a cosmopolitan and varied programme. A movie museum provides a general view of the beginnings of the cinema and there are regular showings of worthwhile old movies or films of artistic or historic interest (see Practical Information – Tourist Information for programme). Since 1973 Brussels has also hosted a Film Festival which is gaining an international following.

Theatre and Cinema

Brussels is Belgium's major centre for music and also fares well internationally in this field. Four large symphony orchestras are based in Brussels: Orchestre National de Belgique (ONB/NOB), Orchestre du Théâtre Royal de la Monnaie, Nouvel Orchestre Symphonique de la RTBF and Sinfonieorkest van de

Music and Dance

BRT (the orchestras of both broadcasting systems). The city also has several chamber music ensembles and important choral societies. After a temporary crisis the opera-house (see A to Z, Théâtre Royal de la Monnaie) has regained the status befitting a European capital. The most renowned facilities for training young musicians are at the Conservatoire Royal, where the teaching is by famous professors and which possesses an unrivalled collection of historical musical instruments (see A to Z, Musée Instrumental).

Brussels is famous for its ballet, and Maurice Béjart's 20th Century Ballet company (Ballet du XXieme siècle) is renowned the world over, particularly for its production of modern ballets.

Concours Musical Reine Elisabeth

At regular intervals Brussels provides the venue (in the Conservatoire and the Palais des Beaux-Arts) for one of the world's most exacting music competitions, the Concours Musical Reine Elisabeth for violin, piano and, more recently, composition. The corresponding stagings of the three categories take place in a four-yearly rotation. Numbered among the Brussels prize-winners are some of the greatest musicians of the last 30 years, including David Oistrach, Emil Gilels, Leonid Kogan, Vladimir Ashkenazy, Gidon Kremer, Stoika Milanova, and Miriam Fried.

Commerce and Industry

Brussels has a long tradition of commerce and industry going as far back as the 11th c., when trade flourished at the upper

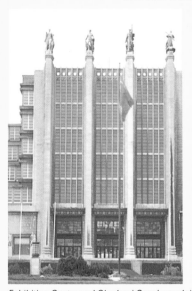

Exhibition Centre and Charleroi Canal – each in its way important for commerce

limit for shipping on the Senne. Brussels was also astride the important international route from Bruges to Cologne, and by the 14th c. was already one of the most important cities for commerce in western Europe. The first half of the 19th c. saw a considerable building-up of communications (railways the Willebroeck Canal, the great boulevards), facilitating early industrialisation of the area around the present Belgian capital. As the centre of the European Community and the seat of top-ranking international and national authorities and organisations (NATO, the National Bank, etc.), Brussels is the metropolis for services in Europe, but industry could also continue to assume a more important role in the city's economy. So far as the labour market is concerned, the major sectors are the building industry, mechanical engineering, textiles, metalworking, foodstuffs, chemicals and printing. Recent years have also seen the growing establishment of the "sunrise industries" (electronics, data-processing, etc.) in the Greater Brussels area.

Famous People

Pieter Bruegel the Elder, who was born in Breda about 1529, was the most important Dutch painter of the 16th c. and even the Expressionists found exciting stimulus in his art.

Pieter Bruegel the Elder (Brueghel, Breughel) (1528/30–69) Dutch painter

His extensive output includes drawings and engravings as well as paintings, but his major creation, which earned him the nickname "Peasant" Bruegel, was the "peasant picture" which was universally popular as a genre in its own right in the 17th and even the 19th c.

What is known of Bruegel's life is based on only a few definite dates and other evidence. His date of birth can be guessed from the fact that he became Master in the Antwerp Guild in 1551, whereupon about 1553 he undertook a journey to Italy that is partly chronicled by engravings and drawings. On his return he worked first in Antwerp then, after his marriage (1563) to Mayken Coecke, daughter of Pieter Coecke of Aelst, he moved to Brussels. This marriage produced both sons, Pieter Bruegel the Younger and Jan the Elder.

An early group of works contains drawings, such as the vast landscapes of 1555, into which he incorporated his impressions of crossing the Alps and whose style was influenced by the Venetian Renaissance painters, particularly Titian and Campagnola. He makes the landscapes, viewed from a high vantage point with few figures in the foreground and bathed in an even light, appear one homogeneous, even universal whole. In his engravings of Christian and Classical attributes, such as "Seven Virtues" (c. 1557) and "Seven Vices" (c. 1558) he sets his depiction of the monstrous, the perverse, of human evil in general, in a landscape broken up into strip-like scenes. Here the iconography employed follows on from the works of Hieronymus Bosch.

In his further works the landscape is no longer a section of the world but a whole world of its own showing the unity of man and his surroundings.

Early on Bruegel was also taking up the topsy-turvy world theme in his first crowd scenes, such as "Dutch Proverbs", "Children's Games" and "The Battle between Carnival and Lent".

A third group of works concurs with the paintings of Hieronymus Bosch, parading the outer limits of human existence – demons and hybrids, part man, part beast, populate a devastated and devastating world. Bloodlust, madness, depravity and fear seem to impel this world of the abyss, examples of this being "The Triumph of Death" (1562/63) and "Dulle Griet" (Mean Maggie, c. 1563).

In other pictures Bruegel achieves a more temperate but just as compelling representative form. In the "Census at Bethlehem" (1566) and the "Massacre of the Innocents" (1565/66) he finds a synthesis with the event in Christ's life being set in what has come to be the traditional representation of the cosmic world view, while its realism is underlined by the depiction of the ordinary, everyday surroundings. His peasant paintings, such as "Peasant Wedding" and "Peasant Dance" (both dating from about 1568) show rustic life and people doing what comes naturally.

Bruegel's works were already prized and sought after throughout Europe during his lifetime; they were collected by Austrian princes and, in Brussels, by Cardinal Granvella. Many of his pictures can be seen in Brussels in the Musée des Beaux-Arts (see A to Z).

André Cluytens
(1905–67)
Belgian-French
conductor

André Cluytens, who was born in Belgium, was a conductor of outstanding importance in the musical life of Brussels. He began his career in music as the Musical Director of a theatre in his home town of Antwerp, where his father was already a conductor. Like so many Belgian musicians before him, he moved on after the Second World War to base himself in Paris. There, for almost two decades, he conducted the greatest orchestras of the French capital and enjoyed a triumphant success with, in particular, the Orchestre de la Société des Concerts du Conservatoire (now the Orchestre de Paris). He came to be so identified with Parisian music life and the music of French composers that people often forgot his Flemish origins, but he also guested regularly in Brussels where he provided the city's music life with some of its most shining hours.

In 1962 Cluytens decided to return to Belgium. He was persuaded to become Chief Conductor of the Belgian National Orchestra (ONB/NOB) which he fomed in a few years into one of Europe's greatest orchestras. The Brussels concerts of this exceptional conductor, who had a special affinity for the works of Beethoven, Brahms and Wagner, as well as Ravel, Debussy, Berlioz and Roussel, became highlights in the eventful history of the Palais des Beaux-Arts (see A to Z).

His untimely death in Paris from a heart attack in June 1967 robbed Brussels of a much-loved musician who shortly before had made his first record with his Brussels orchestra (works of César Franck).

The innumerable recordings made by Cluytens in Berlin, Brussels, Bayreuth, Paris, London and Vienna live on after his death as testimony to the quality of this conductor to whom the musical life of Brussels owes so much.

Pieter Bruegel the Elder   *James Ensor*   *René Magritte*

Paul Delvaux, the internationally acclaimed Surrealist, was born at Antheit near Huy. A Professor at the Royal Academy in Brussels, he is also one of Belgium's most famous contemporary painters.

Paul Delvaux
(b. 1897)
Belgian artist

The son of a lawyer, at his parents' wish he first studied architecture before devoting himself exclusively to painting in 1917. His admiration for his fellow Belgian artists, including James Ensor (see entry), brought him originally under the influence of the Expressionists. Later he was to destroy all his pictures from this period in his search for his own individual style.

The turning-point came in 1932 on a visit to the sideshows at Brussels' Annual Fair. According to Delvaux, it was the Spitzner Waxworks which, amid the hectic gaiety, triggered the artist in him, fascinated as he was by the morbidity and artificiality concealed behind that cheerful façade.

In 1934 he turned to Surrealism under the influence of a Brussels exhibition containing works by Salvador Dali, Max Ernst and Giorgio de Chirico. He started to destroy the familiarity of external reality with Surrealist alienations and absurd arrangements. Henceforth desolate, swept-bare squares with ghostly lighting and yet realistic detailed draughtsmanship in cool shades predominate in his work.

With "Cortège en Dentelle" (Lace Cortege) he set off down his own road where, according to André Breton, he "has turned the whole universe into a single realm in which one woman, always the same women, reigns over the great suburbs of the heart". He sets his female figures – almost always nude or semi-nude – in unreal landscapes and cityscapes, letting them solidify, as in "The Pink Veil" (1937), motionless and incommunicado. "Pygmalion" (1939) also emanates this atmosphere of frozen eroticism, of waxen immobility.

Although about 1944 these figures are confronted by a handsome, clean-cut skeleton, Delvaux did not want this to be taken as a symbol of death, hence his "Venus endormie" (Sleeping Venus). After 1948 railway lines, trains, stations, telegraph poles crop up in the background. The women give the impression of sleepwalkers or dolls. Eroticism is and remains an abstract lure, to which no one knows how to respond.

Besides being an important painter Delvaux is also an equally remarkable graphic artist, whose lithographs and etchings are of the same quality as his oils.

In Brussels Delvaux's work can be seen in the Musées des Beaux-Arts (see A to Z), the Delvaux Collection and the R. Vanthournout Collection.

James Ensor
(1860–1949)
Belgian painter, writer and
composer

James Ensor ranks with Khnopff (see entry) as the foremost representative of Belgian Symbolism, but this is only in terms of the content of his paintings, sculpture and etchings: so far as painting technique and style are concerned, he cannot be said to fall into any of the well-known European categories, despite an undeniable affinity with German Expressionism.

Ensor, whose mother was English, came from Ostend and trained at the Art Academy in Brussels from 1877 to 1880. Brussels is also the theme of his major work "Entry of Christ into Brussels", from a life of Christ that spills over into the fantastic. It is a nightmarish vision of masked mobs and soldiery, an upsurge of social antagonism, of hate and violence, with Christ being greeted in Brussels market-place with banners proclaiming "Vive la Sociale". This picture is imbued with allegory, this being altogether a key-concept for Ensor's work: he was one of the co-founders of Les XX group, with its Symbolist leanings. Also revealed in "Entry of Christ", however, is the legacy of in-depth studies of Pieter Bruegel the Elder (see entry) and Hieronymus Bosch, a feature that becomes increasingly marked in his paintings to the point where they depict weird demonic beings with distorted grimaces and masked features. Ensor's work on display in the Musées Royaux des Beaux-Arts (see A to Z) includes "The Cathedral", probably his most famous etching – a tumult of de-individualised human beings who have turned their backs on a decaying Gothic cathedral, the portrayal of a hell on earth!

Fernand Khnopff
(1858–1921)
Belgian painter and sculptor

"Art is the intoxication of the upper classes" was one of the more snobbish maxims of Fernand Khnopff who, with Ensor (see entry), ranks as the most important representative of Belgian Symbolism.

After studying law and attending Brussels Art College, Khnopff, born the son of a titled family at Grimbergen, near Brussels, went to study in Paris where he was particularly attracted by Eugène Delacroix and Gustave Moreau. This was followed by periods in England and his times with the Pre-Raphaelites, especialy Burne-Jones and Rossetti, while he was also writing for English art periodicals.

Already highly acclaimed in his lifetime, Khnopff's greatest success came at the turn of the century when exhibiting with the Vienna Sezession. Khnopff could also relate to Vienna itself, as a metropolis for the arts whence hailed his ancestors, and as an artist he was strongly influenced by the Viennese form of Art Nouveau (Gustav Klimt).

In 1902 Khnopff had his "dream house" built in Brussels – in white marble in the Viennese Art Nouveau style, with rooms of blue and gold that served as studios as well as living accommodation. Shut away here Khnopff turned out book illustrations, sculpture and paintings, mainly of sphinx-like women who seem withdrawn, aloof, and always appear with the same attributes – a lily and an ivory mask of Hypnos, the god of sleep and brother of death. After 1902 Khnopff led a very secluded life, totally in keeping with his motto, "on n'a que soi" (self is all one has), which he had Tiffany engrave on the lapis lazuli glass sides of his Altar to Hypnos. This studied Decadent and aesthete died in complete seclusion in 1921. In the 50 years that followed his art was forgotten; in the 1930s his white dream house gave way to a developer's apartment block.

It was not until the 1970s that Khnopff was rediscovered by the art historians and the art market. His work is experiencing an unparalleled revival in exhibitions, posters and books, and is very well represented in the Musées des Beaux-Arts (see A to Z), which also houses what is probably his greatest work, "L'Art des Caresses", the Sphinx caressing the naked body of a poet.

René Magritte, the great master of Belgian Surrealism, was born in Lessines, Hainaut, the son of a tailor who moved his family to Brussels in 1902 where, apart from three years in France, Magritte made his home for the rest of his life. After his training at the Brussels Art Academy and early attempts at Cubism in 1922, Magritte became acquainted with the work of Giorgio de Chirico, whose way of painting, with its flights from reality but realistic detail, greatly influenced him. From 1927 to 1930 he lived in Perreux-sur-Marne, near Paris, and was in close touch with the Parisian Surrealists.

René Magritte
(1898–1967)
Belgian painter

In July 1930 Magritte returned to Brussels where he became the spiritual focus of his own Surrealist group, and developed his highly personal version of Surrealism.

He primarily achieved the enigmatic and perplexing effect of his pictures by the combination of contrasting and often excluding elements depicted with utter realism, as, for example, a man looking at a mirror in which the reflection is not of his face but of the back of his head.

Magritte thus offers a picture of reality that is realistic in its detail and viewed almost illusionistically; it is realistic for a man to be looking in a mirror; it is also realistic for the back of a man's head to appear in a mirror. But through the juxtaposition of these disparate details the apparently realistic-illusionistical reality is shattered and the reality reveals itself an illusion.

One of the very many deportations and exiles that Karl Marx experienced during his lifetime took him to Brussels in 1845 where he was able to stay with his family until being deported again in 1848.

Karl Marx
(1818–83)
German social theorist

After studying law, history and philosophy in Bonn Marx graduated from Jena University in 1841 *in absentia*. In 1842 he became Editor in Chief of the anti-establishment paper, "Rheinische Zeitung" in Cologne. His critical articles immediately caused a sensation and on 18 March 1843 he found himself forced to resign as Editor "because of the present censorship".

He and his childhood sweetheart, Jenny von Westphalen, were married in June of the same year and moved to Paris shortly afterwards. In 1845 the Prussian Government succeeded in getting them deported from Paris – Marx had published two anti-Prussian articles in the Parisian German periodical "Vorwärts", which was banned after his deportation.

His next stop was in Brussels – a charge of high treason awaited him in Prussia – and he had to undertake not to publish anything about the current political scene. He first lived for a time at 5 rue de l'Alliance and then later in the present Maison du Cygne (see A to Z, Grand'Place). It was during his stay in

Brussels that he first met Friedrich Engels, with whom he wrote and published, in February 1848, the "Communist Manifesto" which, however, failed to find much of an echo in the Revolution going on at the time.

The Revolution and the publication of the "Manifesto" were too much for the generosity of the Bruxellois and the Belgian politicians, and the Marx family was deported from Belgium early in March. Their next moves were to Cologne, Paris and finally, in 1849, to London where Karl Marx died on 14 March 1883, a few weeks after his eldest daughter, Jenny.

Paul Verlaine
(1844–96)
French poet

Brussels proved a fateful city for the French poetic genius Paul Verlaine. Born in Metz, the son of an officer, Verlaine moved to Paris with his parents in 1851 and seemed set on a humdrum career, becoming a civil servant and, after his wedding in 1870, leading a happy married life. A year after the wedding, however, he met Arthur Rimbaud, poet and male prostitute, and a passionate relationship developed. Verlaine became an alcoholic and in 1872 abandoned his wife and his career to wander round northern France, England and Belgium with Rimbaud.

During their stay in Brussels, when the two friends were coming out of the house of the Deux Nègres Verlaine, who was drunk, shot at Rimbaud in a sudden fit of jealousy during one of their many quarrels, and wounded him in the hand. At the ensuing trial in Brussels' Palais de Justice Verlaine was sentenced to two years' imprisonment which he served in Mons from 1873 to 1875.

Those pistol-shots in Brussels became the turning-point in Verlaine's life. Before his friendship with Rimbaud his poetry had led to his being generally numbered among the Parnassians, as with his "Fêtes galantes" (1869), which are rooted in the Rococo bucolic of Pierre de Ronsard and Jean Honoré Fragonard. During his friendship with Rimbaud Verlaine had then developed a style all his own, rendering the verse more musical by abandoning rigid metrical forms, while at the same time bringing out more taboo spiritual moods such as tenderness, ecstasy, obscenity, eroticism. The shooting in the rue de la Colline brought the turning-point – Verlaine rediscovered Catholicism, harked back to scenes of childhood, turned away from free verse, wrote poems which could be termed prayers and which praised God ("Sagesse", 1881).

Verlaine was no longer able to plunge back into the bourgeoisie after his prison sentence, and in 1874 his wife had divorced him. He scraped along as a teacher in England but the dreams of Catholicism he had entertained in prison proved out of his reach when faced with material hardship. Verlaine lived out his declining years largely in taverns, brothels and the workhouse until his death, alone and penniless, in Paris in 1896.

Rogier van der Weyden
(1400–64)
Flemish painter

Rogier van der Weyden was the major Flemish artist of the Renaissance whose first recorded date is 1427 when he completed his apprenticeship in Tournai to Robert Campin, the Master of Flémalle and former pupil of Jan van Eyck. In 1432 van der Weyden became a Master in the Guild and later settled in Brussels where, before 1436, he became the city artist and achieved a great reputation and solid fortune. He visited Rome, Florence, Ferrara and Venice about 1450 at the invitation of their princes, and journeyed to Cologne some 10 years later to paint the "Altar of the Magi" (now in Munich) for St Columba, returning always to Brussels where he died in 1464.

Since none of his works are signed and there are no contemporary sources as to their authorship, it is often difficult to attribute them with absolute certainty, and the "Annunciation" in the Louvre in Paris has been attributed to the Master of Flémalle as well as to Roger van der Weyden. This should not, however, lead one to conclude that van der Weyden was merely a link in the chain of the great Flemish Renaissance painters, and that his style was indistinguishable from that of the Master of Flémalle and Jan van Eyck. What was new about this artist was above all the dramatic nature of his compositions, compared with the almost wholly static nature of the other two painter's figures. In line with the Flemish tradition there is also considerable stress on the naturalistic (and allegorical) representation of interiors.

Rogier van der Weyden is well represented in the Musées Royaux des Beaux-Arts (see A to Z).

History of Brussels

St Vindicien, Bishop of Cambrai, falls ill in Brussels. Legend has it that he founds the city.	695–712
Mention of Brussels, under the name of "Bruocsella", for the first time, in a chronicle of Emperor Otto the Great.	966
A citadel is built on the island of St-Géry.	977
Charles of France, Duke of Lower Lotharingia, resides in St-Géry citadel.	979
The Duke occupies a new castle on Coudenberg Hill.	1041
Brussels' church is dedicated to St Michael.	1047
Brussels gets its first ramparts.	1100
Building of St Michael's Cathedral, later known as St Michel and St Gudule.	1225
A second city wall is built, roughly corresponding to the presentouter boulevards.	1379
Laying of Town Hall foundation-stone.	1403
Reign of Charles the Bold begins.	1467
Birth in Brussels of Andre Vésale, famous physician.	1514
Charles V moves into Coudenberg Castle.	1515
Erasmus of Rotterdam lives in Anderlecht.	1521

History of Brussels

1531	Brussels is named capital of the Spanish Netherlands.
1555	Charles V abdicates in the Palace of Brussels.
1561	Opening of Willebroeck Canal from Brussels to Antwerp.
1568	Executions of Egmont and Hoorn.
1569	Bruegel dies in his house in the Rue Haute.
1599	Entry of Archduke Albrecht and Isabella.
1617	Building of the Rue Neuve 6 years before the Allée Verte.
1695	Bombardment of Grand'Place by French troops under Marshal de Villeroy.
1703	Founding of Brussels Chamber of Commerce.
1713–15	The Southern Netherlands pass to Austria under the Treaties of Utrecht and La Barrière. Rule of Maria-Theresa.
1719	Execution of Francois Anneessens, Guild Elder and ardent fighter for civic freedom.
1731	Coudenberg Castle burns down.
1744	Charles of Lorraine moves into Brussels.
1763	The young Mozart performs in Brussels during a tour of Europe.
1769	Founding of the Brussels Literary Society.
1789	Brabant leads uprising against Austrian rule and a year later proclaims the United States of Belgium.
1794	Beginning of French rule in Belgium.
1803	Napoleon visits Brussels as First Consul.
1814–30	Brussels becomes second capital of the Kingdom of the Netherlands.
1815	Napoleon is defeated at Waterloo; the Treaty of Vienna gives Belgium to the House of Orange.
1830	Belgium declares its independence and Brussels is named capital of the Kingdom.
1831	Leopold of Saxe-Coburg is elected the first King of the Belgians and moves into the capital which has a population of 100,000 (Greater Brussels 140,000).
1834	Founding of the Free University of Brussels by Theodor Verhaegen.
1835	Opening of the first railway line. It connects Brussels with Mechelen.

Charles V assigns the Netherlands to his son Philip II in Brussels

Founding of the Royal Library.	1837
The public stroll along Europe's first shopping arcade, the Galeries St-Hubert (see A to Z).	1846
Opening celebrations of the main boulevards, built partly on marshy soil. Mayor Anspach has the Senne covered over.	1871
Paul Verlaine stays in Brussels.	1872
International Exhibition in the Cinquantenaire Park.	1880
Brussels Exhibition in the Avenue des Nations.	1910
First World War: German troops invade and occupy Belgium following rejection of Germany's ultimatum and stubborn resistance by the Belgian Army. The Belgian Government escapes to Le Havre in France.	1914–18
International Exhibition in the Centenaire Palace at Heysel where the current exhibition site is located.	1935
Second World War: German troops occupy neutral Belgium in 1940. The Cabinet escapes to England. King Leopold III signs the Capitulation on 28 May 1940 and is interned. Brussels is liberated by British troops on 3 September 1944.	1939–45
Belgium joins NATO.	1949

History of Brussels

1951	Swearing-in of King Baudouin I. Founding of the Concours Reine Elisabeth music competition, successor to the Ysaye Concours founded in 1937.
1958	For 6 months the world flocks to the Heysel Park for the World Fair for which the Atomium is built.
1960	Marriage of King Baudouin to Fabiola de Mora y Aragon of Spain.
1963	Language frontiers established between Flemings and Walloons.
1967	NATO makes Brussels its headquarters.
1975	Establishment of three regional parliaments in Brussels, Mechelen (Flanders) and Namur (for Wallonia and the mainly German-speaking areas of East Belgium). Disagreement about the status of Brussels.
1979	Brussels celebrates its millennium.
1980	Belgium celebrates 150 years of independence, overshadowed by a serious economic crisis. The country is also beset by internal political difficulties because of the ongoing language conflict. Parliament gives the go-ahead for regionalisation. Brussels gets special status.
1981	The economic crisis peaks. Disagreement on the status of Brussels persists.
1984	Glittering opening of the richly refurbished Musée d'Art Moderne.
1985	In the course of a tour of Benelux Pope John Paul II visits Brussels at the end of May.

Brussels from A to Z

Abbaye de La Cambre (La Cambre Abbey)

The former Cistercian abbey (founded about 1200, suppressed 1796), lying in a valley between the Ixelles lakes and the Bois de la Cambre, is an oasis of quiet in the big-city hurly-burly of Brussels.

The church and the abbey buildings, together with the terraced French gardens and the surrounding woodland, form an exceptionally picturesque spot (especially attractive when illuminated in the evening).

A monumental portal leads into the symmetrical courtyard surrounded by the church and abbey buildings.

Abbey
The former Gothic abbey buildings were destroyed in the late 16th c. during the Religious Wars and rebuilt in the Baroque style in the 17th/18th c. Today they house the National Geographical Institute (Institut Géographique National) and a School of Architecture and Decorative Arts (Ecole Nationale Supérieure d'Architecture et des Arts Visuels).

The former Abbey Church of Notre-Dame de La Cambre (14th c.) is an elegant Gothic building with a high, narrow nave (54×11 m (177×36 ft)) and Baroque vault. It was renovated

Location
Avenue Emilie Duray
(entrance Square de la
Croix-Rouge)

Bus
71

Trams
23, 32, 90, 94

Opening times
Church: daily 7.15 a.m.–
midday, 3–6 p.m.
Courtyard and gardens freely
accessible

Abbaye de la Cambre, a former Cistercian abbey

La Cambre Abbay's charming French gardens

in the 1930s (new windows) when the Stations of the Cross were also added. The original Gothic cloister, which can be seen from the nave of the church, was rebuilt in 1599 and since 1934 its windows have incorporated the coats of arms of over 40 abbesses and nuns from the nobility.

Anderlecht

See Maison d'Erasme
See Sts-Pierre et Guidon à Anderlecht

**Atomium   A3

Location
Boulevard du Centenaire
(Heysel)

Bus
89

Trams
18, 52, 81, 92, 103

Opening times
daily 9.30 a.m.–6 p.m.
Panorama: mid April–mid
Sep. daily 9.30 a.m.–10 p.m.

This steel and aluminium structure (designed by André Waterkeyn) built for the World Fair of 1958 still attracts many visitors. It represents the structure of an iron crystal molecule magnified 20 billion times, and is regarded as a symbol of the Atomic Age. With an over-all height of 102 m (335 ft), the Atomium consists of 9 spheres each 18 m (59 ft) in diameter connected by escalators in tubes 30 m (98 ft) in length. In the top sphere, from which there is a marvellous view over Brussels and the surrounding area (lift, 5 m (16·4 ft) per second), is a restaurant and in the 3 lower spheres an exhibition on the peaceful uses of nuclear energy and the development of space travel.

The Atomium, designed for the World Fair of 1958 ▶

*Basilique du Sacré Cœur (national church)   B1/2

Location
Plateau de la Basilique, at
the end of the main street
(Boulevard Léopold II)

Buses
49, 87

Trams
19, 103

This huge monumental building in the north of Brussels, visible from afar, is Belgium's national church, erected in honour of the Sacred Heart and of those who have given their lives for their country.

It was conceived by Leopold II for the 75th anniversary of the Belgian State coming into being. Building started in 1905, lasted over 7 decades and only finished in 1970 with the construction of the dome over the transept. During this long building period not only did several architects work on the church, which was originally intended to be Gothic (Paris 1925 – prize-winning model in the south transept), but fashion changed and with it the design. The result is a mixture of different materials and styles.

Particularly noteworthy in the roomy interior (ground-plan in the shape of a Latin cross, 141×107 m (462×351 ft)) are the stained-glass windows by Jean Huet with characters and scenes from the Bible and the history of religion, and the bronze statue (1941) by Georges Minne on the High Altar, which is almost 3 m (9·8 ft) high.

Berlaymont

See Palais Berlaymont

Beersel

See Château de Beersel

*Bibliothèque Royale Albert Ier (Albertinum)   D3
et Mont des Arts (Albert I Royal Library)

Location
Boulevard de L'Empereur 4

Metro station
Gare Centrale

Buses
20, 29, 34, 38, 65, 66, 71,
95, 96

Trams
92, 93, 94

When King Albert I, founder of the National Fund for Scientific Research, died in February 1934 there was a nation-wide desire to erect a monument in his memory. Three months later King Leopold III suggested to the Prime Minister, Count de Broqueville, that this monument should take the form of a national library. A law passed on 18 March 1935 set up a fund to build the Albert Library. After Parliament ratified the project in 1935 a site had to be found which was in the centre of Brussels and easily accessible.

After much indecision the choice finally fell in 1936 on the Mont des Arts (Mount of the Arts), whereupon an architectural competition was opened on 4 January 1937. This was to be not only for building a library, but also for laying out the extensive associated complex which was to consist of the statue of the King, the royal Museums of Fine Arts (see Palais des Beaux-Arts), the State Archives, the Coin and Print Collection and the offices that went with them. The view, the façades of the Royal Library overlooking the Place de Musée (Museum Square), the

Belgium's national church: Basilique du Sacré Cœur ▶

Mont des Arts with the Congress Building

former apartments of Charles of Lorraine and the Protestant Chapel had to be preserved. After more uncertainty – it had been decided, because of lack of funds, to build the library instead of the greenhouses for the Botanical Gardens and new competition entries had been invited – the choice finally fell on the Mont des Arts in October 1939.

The architects Ghobert and Hoyoux were commissioned to submit their plans. This did not happen, however, until July 1945, after the war. Three famous English, Dutch and French architects were consulted and thought the plans excellent.

Mont des Arts

The present-day Mont des Arts warrants a description. The central portion is in line with an axis that runs from the Church of Saint-Jacques-sur-Coudenberg through the statues of Godefroy de Bouillon and King Albert to the tower of the Town Hall (see Grand'Place).

The little Rue du Musée (Museum Street) has been widened to 15 m (49 ft). It is entered through an archway from which there is a view over the beautiful Museum Square and the former Royal Library.

Opposite the fine old Hôtel Ravenstein are the two wings of the Congress Hall which has been a lively venue since the 1958 World Fair. The two wings are separated by a gap of 28 m (92 ft) which affords a view of the statue. On either side are the monumental entrances, with an arcade of fine shops running along one side.

Garden

In the centre of the complex there are carefully tended gardens

Royal Library   *Place Royale: Godefroy de Bouillon*

with the equestrian statue of King Albert I. From the top a flight of steps leads to a terrace and gives access to a promenade of over 100 m (107 yd) along the two wings of the Congress Hall. On both sides of the terrace huge flights of steps lead to the gardens. This quiet spot is ornamented with high reliefs and a fountain.

Royal Library (Albertinum)

The main building containing the book collection is in Rue de Ruysbroeck. There are almost 100 km (62 miles) of shelves, which can be extended by a further 20–25 km (12–16 miles) if required. The earlier library had only 45 km (28 miles) of shelves. Almost 3 million volumes are kept here in all.

A special feature is a framework of small very closely ordered pillars designed to act as both building and shelving supports. Everything is geared to the best possible way of preserving the books: even the lighting conditions have been taken into account. A system of pneumatic tubes ensures that readers get a prompt service; it takes barely six minutes from a book being ordered to its arrival in the reader's hands – a truly record achievement.

Below the lecture theatre are strong-rooms, with walls and ceilings of reinforced concrete, in which the rare books and valuable paintings of the Musée d'Art Ancien (Royal Museum of Ancient Art) can be safely housed in times of danger.

Apart from the tastefully furnished exhibition rooms the library also contains numerous reading-rooms set aside for those consulting specialist material, manuscripts, rare and valuable books, catalogues, etc.

Bois de la Cambre

Bibliothèque de Bourgogne
The Bibliothèque de Bourgogne, with is precious manuscripts and treasure store of rare books, old maps and plans, is housed in the Albertinum cellars in a spacious, specially climatically controlled strong-room.

---

*Bois de la Cambre

Location
5 km (3 miles) SE of the city centre

Trams
32, 94

Buses
51, 71

The lovely park of Bois de la Cambre is to the people of Brussels rather like the Bois de Boulogne is to the Parisians. The actual Bois de la Cambre, covering as it does only 124 ha (306 acres), is in fact considerably smaller that its Paris counterpart, but it virtually joins on to the Forêt de Soignes (see entry) so that together they make up an extensive area of park and woodland. The Bois de la Cambre extends over slightly hilly and partly wooded terrain and contains a small lake (boat hire). Restaurants, play areas, walks and sporting facilities in the immediate vicinity attract thousands of visitors, especially at week-ends.

Avenue Louise

Until as late as 1842 the site of the present park was part of the Forêt de Soignes. In that year Brussels, seeking a "green lung", annexed the site and commissioned the landscape-gardener Keilig to lay out an imposing park. To get there, however, the Bruxellois had to negotiate well-nigh impassable terrain for a further two decades, since for a long time the communes of Ixelles and St-Gilles, who owned the land between the present Boulevard Extérieur and the Bois de la Cambre, blocked what

Bois de la Cambre: woods and parkland on Brussels' doorstep

they saw as Brussels' "craving to expand". Not until 1864 did a regulation enable the building of the splendid Avenue Louise, which forms a direct and speedy route from the city centre to the Bois de la Cambre. The Avenue Louise was thus originally an elegant promenade used by the Bruxellois to get out into the countryside. This also explains the curious fact that the Avenue Louise and the Bois de la Cambre still belong to the Commune de Bruxelles and not to Ixelles, St-Gilles or Uccle to which geographically speaking they ought to belong. However as all four communes are now incorporated in Greater Brussels (Agglomération de Bruxelles) the problem is no longer relevant.

Along the east side of the Bois de la Cambre runs the Avenue Franklin D. Roosevelt with its elegant mansions, embassies and the old administration building and the lecture theatres of Brussels Free University. Most of the University's institutes and lecture theatres were relocated 2 km (1½ miles) north-east on the site of the former Champ de Manœuvres (drill ground) in Etterbeek.

Avenue F. D. Roosevelt

Botanical Gardens

See Domaine de Bouchout

*Botanique (Centre Culturel de la Communauté Française)   C4

Between the Place Rogier (see entry) and the Porte de Schaerbeek is the 6·4 ha (15·8 acre) former Botanical Garden, laid out between 1826 and 1829. Its old glasshouses have been thoroughly renovated in recent years and house the Cultural Centre of the French Community in Brussels which opened in 1984. Two theatres, a cinema, several exhibition rooms, a library and facilities for other cultural activities together with a constantly changing programme attract large numbers of visitors every day.

Location
Place Rogier/Porte de Schaerbeek

Metro station
Botanique

Opening times
daily 10 a.m.–midnight

Boulevards   C/D2–4

The Inner Boulevards (Boulevards du Centre), laid out between 1867 and 1874, in part above the vaulted bed of the Senne, cut through the Old Town roughly between the North Station and the South Station parallel to the older line of streets formed by Rue Neuve (see entry) and Rue de Midi.

Boulevards du Centre (Inner Boulevards)

The Boulevards Adolphe Max and Emile Jacqmain run from the Boulevard du Jardin Botanique about on a level with Place Rogier (see entry) to merge into the spacious Place de Brouckère. The Anspach Monument, a 20 m, (66 ft) high fountain, commemorates Mayor Jules Anspach (1863–79), the man chiefly responsible for promoting the boulevards; the fountain used to stand in the centre of this square but has been removed and re-erected in the fish market.

Place de Brouckère

Boulevards

A lot of important town-planning measures in recent years have decisively altered the face of the Place de Brouckère. Modern commercial buildings and shopping arcades (Centre Monnaie, Philips, Anspach Center) have replaced the old *fin-de-siècle* buildings that once made the square strongly reminiscent of Paris.

Boulevard Anspach

Together with the Boulevard Adolphe Max and the Rue Neuve the Boulevard Anspach which terminates in the square, is one of the liveliest streets in the city, at least as far as the Place de la Bourse. This is where the imposing Stock Exchange building (see Bourse) is located.

On the far side of the Stock Exchange opposite the Rue des Pierres, whose Flemish name, Steenstraat, recalls a medieval castle, the Rue du Borgval (castle mound) runs to the right to the Place St-Géry with its covered market. This is on the site of the former Isle of St-Géry, the cradle of the old city. Just to the south stands the Church of Notre-Dame aux Riches-Claires (see entry). Farther south-east, on the other side of the Boulevard Anspach, is the Church of Notre-Dame de Bon-Secours (see entry).

The Boulevard Anspach is continued by the Boulevard Maurice Lemonnier which ends at the Place de la Constitution, not far from the South Station (Gare du Midi).

Particularly impressive is an evening stroll along the Inner Boulevards, especially from the Bourse to the Place Rogier, when the Boulevard and the Place de Brouckère, illuminated by a host of advertising signs and large-scale streetlighting, look like a metropolitan sea of lights.

Place de Brouckère

Boulevard Anspach

34

Boulevards Extérieurs (Ceinture; Outer Boulevards)

The 8 km (5 miles) of Boulevards enclosing the pentagon of the old city of Brussels, called Outer Boulevards or even Ceinture in contrast to the Inner Boulevards (see Boulevards du Centre), were laid out between 1818 and 1840 on the site of the former 14th c. city walls. At the busiest junctions the very heavy traffic flow is facilitated by underpasses and viaducts.

The north-east boulevard, the Boulevard du Jardin Botanique, runs past the Place Rogier (near the North Station – see entry) and leads to the Upper Town. On the left are what were formerly the Botanical Gardens (see Botanique).

Boulevard du Jardin Botanique

The Boulevard Bischoffsheim continues on the far side of the junction with the Rue Royale (on the left is the striking social insurance tower block of Prévoyance Sociale). At the north end of the Rue Royale can be seen the dome of the Church of Ste-Marie, built between 1845 and 1853 in the Romanesque-Byzantine style. It lies in the suburb of Schaerbeek, the commune with the highest population in Greater Brussels.

Boulevard Bischoffsheim

The Place Madou, with its 31-storey tower block is the starting-point for the busy Boulevard du Régent, which meets the Rue de la Loi not far from the Palais de la Nation and then passes through the elegant districts of the city near the Parc de Bruxelles and the Quartier Léopold (left). On the right between the Boulevard and the Park stands the Palais des Académies (see entry), built between 1823 and 1829 for the then Prince of Orange. Farther along on the right is the Place du Trône with an equestrian statue of Leopold II dating from 1925; behind is the garden of the Royal Palace.
The Boulevard du Régent ends near the square called Porte de Namur where it meets busy streets leading from the city centre to Ixelles.

Boulevard du Régent

The broad double artery of the Boulevard de Waterloo and the Avenue de la Toison d'Or carry a lot of traffic between the Porte de Namur in the north-east and the Porte de Hal (see entry) in the south-west. At the Place Louise the Avenue Louise branches off southwards to the Bois de la Cambre.
These three streets and the arcades leading off from them today form the Upper Town's exclusive shopping district. Gucci, Chanel, Louis Féraud, Daniel Hechter, Van Cleef and Arpels are only some of the names that guarantee that anything bought here will be expensive and of good quality. There are also several luxury hotels and restaurants in this area.

Boulevard de Waterloo, Avenue de la Toison d'Or, Avenue Louise

The boulevards leading north from the Porte de Hal offer hardly anything worth seeing and serve primarily to carry through traffic.

North-west Boulevards

Bourse (Stock Exchange)   C3

La Bourse, the stock exchange building, in the Place de la Bourse half-way between the North and South Stations, is Belgium's most important stock exchange ahead of Antwerp, Ghent and Liège.
The Brussels Stock Exchange was founded as a result of an

Location
Place de la Bourse

Metro station
Bourse

Bourse

La Bourse, Belgium's most important stock exchange

Buses
34, 48, 95, 96

Façade

agreement made on 19 Messidor of Year IX following the French Revolution, that is on 8 July 1801. The Government in Paris first sited it in the former Augustinian monastery and it was subsquently moved many times before finally being relocated on the new inner-city North-South boulevard.

The Classical-style building, which is based on a design by the architect L. Suys, stands quite apart and is richly decorated. The façade is formed by a colonnade preceded by a broad flight of open steps. Six Corinthian columns surmounted by the cornice, which bears the inscription "Bourse de Commerce", support the triangular pediment. A bas-relief (the work of J. Jacquet) represents "noble" Belgium surrounded by figures symbolising Industry (right) and Shipping (left). The attic (parapet wall) above the pediment is highly ornamental, and right at the top towers Jacquet's figure of Belgium, accompanied by the two symbolic figures of Trade and Industry, with, below it, the escutcheon of Belgium framed by a massive garland. At each end of the arch is a group representing Trade on Land (right) and Trade by Water (left). Two sleeping lions, one at each side, complete the decoration of the frontage. They are the work of the sculptor Elias.

At the top of the steps rise three splendid portals. Over the main door, surrounding the clock, are two winged figures symbolizing Good and Evil, by De Haen. A vaulted pediment towers above the ground-floor window and bears two figures representing Post and Telegraphy (right) and Work and Prosperity (left). At the sides of the steps two lions (by Jacquet) are each led by a Genius holding a blazing torch.

Inside the Stock Exchange

The south façade on the Rue Henri Maus is dominated by the central section, designed by the architect Brunfaut, and its most impressive features are the Corinthian columns, a garlanded cornice and the Brussels coat of arms in the tympanum.

South façade

The outer sections are brought together in the centre by the main building, with the ends strongly projecting. The surface is bedecked with symbolic figures – on the right, holding a cockerel, is Vigilance and on the left are Art and Knowledge by G. De Groot. On the attic are two groups consisting of three figures by the sculptor A. J. van Rasbourgh representing Asia and Africa. Between the two storeys is a frieze designed by Carrier-Belleuse, in conjunction with Rodin and J. Dillens.

The rear face is in the same style as the façade. It contains two figures by the sculptor Samain representing Trade and Shipping; in the centre a winged Genius by Jacquet; at the ends of the attic two groups of children, on the right "Trade" by E. Melot, on the left "Working in the Fields" by J. van Den Kerkhove. The frieze by Carrier-Belleuse separates the two storeys.

The north façade overlooking the Rue de la Bourse echoes the arrangement of the south façade but the sculptures have different themes. Opposite the Church of St-Nicholas (see entry) G. De Groot has symbolized Agriculture. Towards the Place de la Bourse is his work "Metalurgy". "America" and "Europe" by van Oemberg decorate the vaulted surface of the attic. Over the window gables are allegorical figures corresponding to those already seen.

North façade

The two storeys are separated by the frieze with numerous reliefs.

Brigittines' Church

See Notre-Dame de la Chapelle

*Brussels Lace

Brussels was an important centre for the manufacture of lace as early as the second half of the 16th c. Brussels lace, also known as Brabant lace, was in very great demand abroad, particularly in Paris and with the suppliers to the French Court.

18th c.

A reliable report states that in the 18th c. Brussels, where numerous manufacturers were based, had 10,000 women making lace. This century was the Golden Age of Brussels lace, with orders streaming in from the ruling households. It is sometimes possible to tell from surviving lacework which noble household or which monarch it was intended for. A very fine robe kept in the Museum of Costume and Lace bears the monogram of Emperor Charles VI and the insignia of the Order of the Golden Fleece with, on guard, the Imperial crowned eagle. This magnificent garment was undoubtedly made for a lavish ceremony, the obvious one being the Proclamation of the Pragmatic Sanction whereby Charles VI ensured that his daughter Maria-Theresa could succeed to the Imperial throne. The influence of the French style can be seen in 18th c. lace-making – about 1750 there are the fantastic Rococo and Oriental motifs that call for incredible virtuosity on the part of their makers. In the first half of the century lace-making was an art very much in demand, with bonnets, bodices, ruffs, bows, cuffs and even whole garments being made of it.

Brussels lace was the most sought after because of the fineness of its thread and the beauty of the designs. Today it is still possible to follow, in the museums, the development of the art of lace-making and to admire the exceptional skill of its creators. Their creativity was inspired by flora and fauna: roses, carnations, peonies, narcissi, deer and squirrels, dolphins spouting water, fountains and shells are subtly incorporated into the pattern of the lace in a way that was never to be seen again.

At that time, when everything was ruled by fashion, even the religious scenes on the beautiful Confirmation veils and the robes of the holy statues were hardly any less worldly. Some of these, such as the head-dress of Our Lady of Loreto (Eglise des Minimes) and the lace of Our Lady in Notre-Dame de Laeken (see entry) are found in Brussels churches. The Béguine veil in the Royal Museum of Art and History (see Palais du Cinquantenaire), which shows a princess kneeling in the park, presumably represents a scene from the legend of the founding of the Béguine Order by St Begga.

The art of lace-making in Belgium reached its peak in the 18th c. Some maintain that the Brussels school created English Point (Point d'Angleterre), which was in great demand and, therefore, very expensive. Others maintain that this was lace that had been smuggled in and which caused Brussels lace to be called English lace which, though it fooled nobody, eventually came to be the term accepted in France and even in Brussels.

According to a 1745 publication, "Brussels lace is beautiful to

A lace-maker at work

behold and everywhere popular. It keeps the fair sex occupied. Some work on it as a pastime, others of necessity, and there are so to speak as many making this dainty ware as there are private houses."

Mechelen was just as renowned for lace as the future capital city, and had a considerable lace trade.

About 1770, however, lace gradually lost its popularity. During the last quarter of the 18th c. the lace-makers left the towns, the art of lace-making declined and finally lost its greatest admirers.

The Revolution came as a blow to lace. Men ceased to give it their custom. Nevertheless the lace industry came alive again. Napoleon was particularly keen on Brussels lace and ordered large quantities of it. 19th c.

In the 19th c., however, lace-making ceased to evolve. People appeared to be content with imitating past achievements, without bothering about the schools that were always on the look out for new patterns. This decline was exacerbated by the invention of machine-made tulle which was much cheaper to produce than hand-made work. Fashions changed from year to year and interest in fine old lace dwindled.

The new technique allowed flowers and motifs that had been made separately to be appliquéd on. This was the technique used in producing the lace pictures, in the style of David, representing Apollo and Daphne, Mars and Venus, and the huge bedspread with the coat of arms of the Russian Tsars in the Costume and Lace Museum.

The 19th c. also saw the rise to fashion of sewn Brussels lace, also known as Point de Gaze (gauze stitch) because of its delicacy, and Duchess lace in honour of Queen Marie-

Brussels Lace

Henriette when she was still Duchess of Brabant. This was bobbin lace interspersed with medallions.

As well as these types of lace, which are no longer made today, there finally appeared the Rosaline, which can still be bought and which occasionally harks back to the delicate designs of the early 18th c.

Trading regulations

A few rare edicts, letters and traders' accounts relating to sales or customs duties provide information on lace-making, prices and exports to England, France, Spain, Russia, etc.

From the 17th c. onwards there were strict measures aimed at preventing the lace-makers from emigrating and at anyone helping them to do so, as well as any attempts to take Brussels lace out of the country. England, with an astonishingly high demand for lace, gave shelter to the runaways but was never able to compete with lace made in Brussels. This would have required business expertise, but despite tempting offers from rival nations no Brussels manufacturer was ever lured to leave.

Famous pieces of lacework

Head-dress of Our Lady in Notre-Dame du Sablon:

Outstanding among all the magnificent pieces of Brussels lace in the city's churches and museums is the wonderful head-dress of Our Lady, dating from the second half of the 17th c., in the Church of Notre-Dame du Sablon (see entry). It depicts the boat in which, according to legend, the Virgin Mary sailed from Antwerp to Brussels where her arrival is said to have given rise to the Ommegang (see Practical Information – Calendar of Events). The parrots embroidered on the tracery of boughs surrounding it, together with the Virgin's monogram, refer to another legend, that of the parrot that was taught to say "Mary" and thus was saved from the claws of a falcon.

Eiderdown of Albert I and Isabella:

The Royal Museum of Art and History (see Palais du Cinquantenaire) houses a masterpiece of astonishing beauty, a pictorial witness of the past: the eiderdown that was presented to Grand Duke Albert and Grand Duchess Isabella on the occasion of their marriage and enthronement as Duke and Duchess of Brabant.

This incomparable piece has been researched but the iconographic questions it poses have never been satisfactorily answered. The 120 scenes round the edge show the Ommegang procession (see Practical Information – Calendar of Events), but there is no saying whether it is that of a particular town or one specially organised in honour of the new rulers. The various monograms and coats of arms bespeak the couple's relationship to the Archdukes, and the figure of St Gudula together with the fact that the eiderdown was made in Brabant give rise to the assumption of a link with Brussels. Made entirely of bobbin lace, it has many of the special features that distinguish Brussels lace, especially the method of emphasising reliefs and the skilful technique of working sections into the tulle, whereby the motifs are made separately and braided or stitched together by hand, a procedure calling for outstanding skill on the part of the lace-makers and organisational ability on the part of the person supervising them. This method enables large pieces such as gowns, bedspreads and eiderdowns to be made in a short time. Yet here in the completed work all the individual achievements are submerged into the anonymity of the perfect unit formed by this

Brussels lace, famed the world over ▶

outstanding work as a whole. No mark, no signature, nothing except the piece itself immortalises its designer and the people who made it.

Present-day lace

Although nowadays the price of lace is said to be prohibitive, it has always been an extremely costly item which has kept its value compared with other articles in everyday use. The reason for the decline in the art of lace-making is to be sought not so much in the price of lace as in the sweeping social change that has brought with it a radically different concept of luxury and the outward trappings of wealth. Furnishings and clothing are subject only to the dictates of comfort and hygiene, running counter to a technique that has finally been dethroned by machine-made imitations.

Despite this Belgian lace still has a faithful following abroad where it meets with a liking and awareness that keep alive the fame of the deft lace-makers overseas. Hence in the summer lace-makers in their traditional costumes can still be seen outside souvenir shops in Ghent, Brussels and Bruges assiduously plying their nimble craft under the fascinated gaze of the tourists.

Despite the stiff competition by which it is threatened from hand-made goods from the Far East and machine-manufacturing, this ancient luxury industry keep up its traditions. It is still alive and well in Bruges, Turnhout and throughout northern Belgium where the traditional designs have been adapted to modern tastes to continue producing the finest and most valuable lace items.

Exports, which once exceeded 25 million and then suffered a serious setback because of the world economic crisis, are again on the increase, and buyers are once more tending to insisit on having lace of the best quality.

If one considers, however, that shortly before the turn of the century Belgium had almost 50,000 lace-makers, in particular in the Flemish districts, the current resurgence seems unimpressive, but it is sufficient to allow for the hope that, despite the Machine Age, the lace-maker's calling will not die out completely.

Centre Cultural de la Communauté Française

See Botanique

*Château de Beersel (Beersel moated castle)

Location
10 km (6 miles) S

Tram
55 to Uccle-Calevoet, then bus UB

Just south of Brussels, near the little village of Beersel, is the interesting moated castle of Château de Beersel. This pretty simicircular brick building with its three towers dates from the early 14th c. and, thanks to sympathetic restoration, retains its ancient splendour.

Housed on the ground floor of the highest tower is a small museum (torture chamber, etc.).

Huizingen

Huizingen Park (92 ha (227 acres)) a little farther south has leisure and camping facilities, mini-golf, open-air swimming-pool, youth hostel, etc.

Château de Rivieren (Rivieren Castle)

The Château de Rivieren at Ganshoren is a charming little castle, built in the 16th and 17th c. Its graceful silhouette is picturesquely reflected in the water-filled moat.
The lovely park that surrounds the castle invites the visitor to linger.

Location
Ganshoren, Avenue du Château

*Château Royal de Laeken (Laeken Royal Palace)   A3/4

The residence of the King of the Belgians, set amid 160 ha (395 acres) of wooded parkland in the north of Brussels, is an unpretentious Classical building of noble proportions constructed between 1782 and 1784 for the Governor at that time and renovated following a fire in 1890.
In front of the palace is a monument with a statue of King Leopold I, from which there is a magnificent view of the Belgian capital.

Location
Avenue du Parc Royal
B1020 (Laeken)

Bus
53

Trams
52, 92

The famous Royal Greenhouses (Serres Royales), which have been recently renovated, were built for Leopold II, a gardening enthusiast, who made them the focus of his artistically fashioned park. The greenhouses and their beautiful plants are open to the public once a year, usually a fortnight in May.

Royal Greenhouses

At the north edge of the park stands the Japanese Tower and opposite it (entrance Avenue J. van Praet) the Chinese

Chinese Pavilion (Museum)

The Chinese Pavilion – opposite Laeken Palace

Pavilion, brought here from the 1900 World Fair in Paris, which houses collections of Asiatic art, especially Chinese porcelain (open Tues.–Sun. 9.30 a.m.–12.30 p.m., 1.30–5 p.m.).

Japanese Tower

Originally an exhibit at the 1900 World Fair in Paris, the Japanese Tower was re-erected in the park at Laeken in 1901–04 by King Leopold II.

Stuyvenberg Estate

The Stuyvenberg Estate in the west part of Laeken Park dates from the early 16th c. It was enlarged in the 18th c. and the pretty little palace was the dowager house of Queen Elisabeth from 1951 until her death.

Colonne du Congrès (Congress Column) C4

Location
Place du Congrès between Parc de Bruxelles and Jardin Botanique

Bus
38

Trams
92, 93, 94

This monument, 47 m (154 ft) high over all, was built in 1859 to commemorate the National Congress that proclaimed the Belgian Constitution after the 1830 Revolution.

The foundation-stone was laid in the presence of King Leopold I in September 1850 and the work was entrusted to the architect Poelaert, who had also designed the Palais de Justice (see entry).

The 25 m (82 ft) high column is surmounted by a statue of King Leopold I while the Eternal Flame burns in honour of the Unknown Soldier at its base.

From the esplanade around the Congress Column there is a fine panoramic view, with the modern buildings of the Cité administrative in the foreground.

*Domaine de Bouchout (Jardin Botanique National de Belgique)

Location
14 km (9 miles) N of the city centre near Meise

Bus
55

The new Jardin Botanique National de Belgique (Botanical Gardens) was officially opened on the site of the Bouchout Estate in 1958. The gardens and greenhouses are grouped around a 12th c. moated castle, which had served as the residence of Leopold II's sister, Empress Charlotte of Mexico, after having been restored in the 19th c.

In addition to a host of rare plants the Botanical Gardens also accommodate important scientific facilities such as an extensive specialist library, laboratories and a wide variety of herbariums.

*Domaine de Gaasbeek (Gaasbeek Château and grounds)

Location
14 km (9 miles) SW

Tram
LK from Place Rouppe

This medieval château at Gaasbeek south-west of Brussels has been State-owned since 1921 and is one of the favourite spots for outings by the Bruxellois.

Parts of the château date from the 13th c. and others from the 16th c. It belonged at one time to Count Egmont, hero of the Dutch Resistance who also spent the last years of his life here. The interior of the château houses a museum displaying old furniture, tapestries, goldenware and carvings in wood and ivory.

Park

Visitors can go for invigorating walks in the fine 40 ha (100 acre) park around the château.

Gaasbeek Château, a favourite outing for the Bruxellois

European Community

See Palais Berlaymont

Flea Market (Marché aux Puces or Vieux Marché)   D3

The Brussels flea market lies in the quarter known as Les Marolles (see entry) – at the foot of the Palais de Justice (see entry) – and stretches as far as Notre-Dame de la Chapelle (see entry), the church containing the tomb of Pieter Bruegel the Elder. The painter lived close by in the Rue Haute, the parallel street to the Rue Blaes, both of which traverse the Marolles quarter.

Threadbare trousers, laddered stockings and down-at-heel shoes, nails and screws, pieces of china – some cracked and some not, pictures, books, carpets, bits of old wireless sets, bikes, prams, coins, stamps, musical instruments, spectacles, old money-boxes, cages, clock parts, rusty keys, records and cookers, old ties, curtains, furs next to old engines, a jumble of all kinds of rags and tatters, heaps of old weapons, medals and helmets, maps and magazines, china from washstands and dolls with no hair, in other words, there is nothing that you won't come across in one form or another in Brussels flea market. Not long ago you could still find Iron Crosses from both world wars.

Like the whole quarter, this market, where the dealers lay out their junk on the paving-stones of the square, is absolutely

Location
Place du Jeu de Balle

Buses
20, 48

Opening times
daily 8 a.m.–1 p.m.

A corner of Brussels flea market

unique, and, especially on Sunday mornings, it has a clientele all of its own who come looking for rarities. There are bargains to be had here, and the people buying them are a fruitful study in themselves.

Lost keys can be replaced on the spot by the locksmith who has set up his stall and workbench at the side of the road, while at other stalls there are cycles and motor bikes being mended or sold – here every spare part is obtainable.

The Bruxellois like coming to look round the flea market on Sunday mornings because that is when it is at its height. They cherish the secret hope that one day they will turn up something splendid that they can actually use or enjoy.

Forest

Location
S on the slopes of the Senne

Buses
48, 50

The suburb of Forest, with its strikingly regular street pattern and broad expanses of greenery, lies on the slopes of the Valley of the Senne.

The lovely 13 ha (32 acre) Parc de Forest was laid out in 1878 to a design by V. Besme.

Farther south is the 23 ha (57 acre) Parc Duden which once belonged to a monastery and is now named after its last private owner.

St-Gilles
Musée Horta

North of Forest is the suburb of St-Gilles with its imposing town hall and, in the Rue Américaine, the Musée Horta, the museum of one of the most important architects in Art Nouveau.

See St-Denis à Forest

Forêt de Soignes, among Belgium's finest woodland

*Forêt de Soignes

South-east of Brussels on the far side of the Bois de la Cambre (see entry) is the Forêt de Soignes (Soignes Forest), covering some 5000 ha (9880 acres), which, with its magnificent groves of beeches, is one of Belgium's finest woodlands.

Location
SE Greater Brussels

Tram
44

The village of Groenendael lies in a valley in the centre of the forest, which has several excellent roads running through it. Located 13 km (8 miles) from the city centre (leave via the Porte de Namur, drive through Ixelles and Boisfort then take the 430), Groenendael was once the site of the famous Augustinian abbey founded in 1343 by the mystic Ruysbroek. The only building still standing, which dates from the 18th c., now houses the exclusive Château de Groenendael restaurant. On the north side of the valley is the Arboretum de Groenendael with over 400 types of tree and shrub and a forestry museum.

Groenendael

Seven kilometres (4·5 miles) south-east of Groenendael on the far side of the Forêt de Soignes lies the pretty summer resort of Genval with its medicinal spring and several nearby lakes. Some 3 km (2 miles) farther east is the village of Rixensart with the château of the Counts of Merode (1631–62).

Genval

The ruins of the 14th c. Abbey of Rouge-Cloître in the north part of the forest, where it merges with the Tervuren Woods, are a popular rendezvous for artists.

Rouge-Cloître Abbey

Façade and interior of the Galeries Saint-Hubert

* Galeries Saint-Hubert (shopping arcade)   C3

Location
Between Rue du Marché-
aux-Herbes and Rue de
l'Ecuyer

Metro stations
Gare Centrale, Bourse

Buses
29, 63, 65, 66, 71

The Galeries Saint-Hubert, a long covered gallery with shops,
cafés and restaurants, was Europe's first shopping arcade.
Built in 1845 by a Brussels company formed especially for the
purpose, it was designed by the architect Jean-Pierre
Chuisenaer and the foundation-stone was laid by King
Leopold I on 6 May 1846.
It runs for 200 m (219 yd) parallel to the Boulevard du Centre
and splits up into the Galerie du Roi (King's Arcade) at the Rue
de l'Ecuyer end and the Galerie de la Reine (Queen's Arcade)
at the Rue du Marché-aux-Herbes end. In front of it is the
magnificent Rue de la Colline with its picturesque gables. The
Rue du Marché-aux-Herbes on the right has several alleys
branching off it (some of them culs-de-sac) and in the
background is 'Brussels' front room', the Grand'Place (see
entry).

Façade

The façade, inspired by Classical architecture, is decorated with
overlapping pilasters and has statues in the niches. A bas-relief
shows the head of Mercury surrounded by two rivers. The
motto "Omnibus omnia" (everything to everyone) was taken
from the old silversmith's house that used to stand here.

Interior

The interior is decorated with imitations of the busts and
statuettes that can be seen on the façade (by Jacquet). Near the
clock are allegorical figures representing Belgium, Brabant and
the City of Brussels.
At the corner of Rue des Bouchers (Butchers' Street) and the

Galerie de la Reine are two plaques commemorating the 50th and 100th anniversaries of its construction.
On 7 Galerie du Roi is a commemorative plaque with the inscription 'Here on 1 March 1896 the first public performance of a cinematographic picture show took place.' Today the cinema is in the Galerie de la Reine; it is also used as a theatre. In 1851 Victor Hugo's mistress Juliette Drouot lived in the little Galerie des Princes (Princes' Arcade), which branches off from the Galerie du Roi.

Grand'Place (market place)   C3

In the centre of the Old Town lies the Grand'Place (110 m (120 yd) by 68 m (74 yd)), Brussels' market place, with the town hall and the guildhalls. Entirely medieval, it is one of the most beautiful squares in the world and makes a delightful picture any time of the day and in the evening particularly. Although most of the houses were rebuilt in the Baroque style after the bombardment of 1695, the square still possesses its inimitable monumental character and represents a happy blend of Gothic and Baroque.

Metro stations
Bourse, Gare Centrale

Buses
29, 34, 48, 65, 66, 71, 95, 96

Town Hall (Hôtel de Ville, Stadhuis)

At the peak of its commercial and political power, Brussels decided about 1440 to build a town hall that in its splendour and magnificence would surpass the one Bruges had begun to build in 1370. Originally it was envisaged there would only be the left wing, built between 1402 and 1410, with the Lion Steps forming the main entrance and flanked on its right by an existing tower, the Belfried.
The Town Hall is one of the oldest buildings in the Flemish style. It was rebuilt after the French bombardment in 1695 which left only the tower and the rough stonework standing. It owes its present appearance, both externally and internally, to the renovation work begun in 1841 and continued in the early 20th c.

The architect was probably Jacques van Thienen from Tienen. The doors of the colonnade lead into the ground-floor rooms, which used to house the city police. The colonnade itself provided shelter for the stalls at fair-times.
Above the staircase there are two large reliefs cut into the stone, one showing the murder of the Lay Assessor Everard 't Serclaes by the Count of Gaasbeek (1388) and the other Judge Herkenbald, the Lay Assessor who sentenced and personally executed his own nephew.
The small figures surrounding the portal are typical of the sculpture of the first quarter of the 15th c. The small corner tower on the left had a clock with a dial as early as 1411.
From the first-floor balcony the rulers watched the events being staged in the square and from here decrees were announced to the assembled townsfolk. The Dukes appeared on the balcony after their enthronements to receive the homage of the people.

Left wing

The name of the architect is not known but variations in style show that this wing was built later.
On the capitals of the colonnade are numerous partly satirical carvings dating from about 1450. Their meaning was unknown

Right wing

49

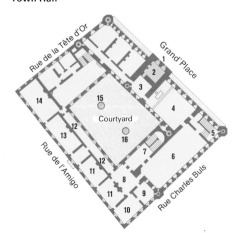

Town hall
Hôtel de Ville
Stadhuis

30 m
100 ft

1 Portal (entrance)
2 Tower (Belfried)
3 Anteroom
4 Registry Office
5 Lion Steps
6 Gothic Hall
7 Ceremonial staircase
8 Mayor's antechamber
9 Secretary's office
10 Mayor's office
11 Lay Assessor's office
12 Portrait gallery
13 Maximilian Hall
14 Council Chamber
15 Scheldt Fountain
16 Maas Fountain

until 1935 when they were found to be the shields of the inns that had been demolished to make way for this wing of the Town Hall.

1st capital: De Scupsteol: the 'Estrapade', a torture in which the victim is ducked in liquid mud.

2nd capital: Papenkelder (Monks' cellar): hard-drinking 'Merry Monks'.

3rd capital: De Moor (the moor): the 'Sleeping Moor' accompanied by his harem.

The originals of these carvings are in Brussels' Municipal Museum (Maison du Roi).

The statues on the façade represent the Dukes and Duchesses of Brabant.

Tower

The tower, a masterpiece of elegance and artistry, is without doubt one of the world's finest monuments and was completed by Jan van Ruysbroek (1454) in what was then the remarkably short timespan of six years.

The tower consists of a square four-storey section, an octagonal three-storey middle section and a tracework pyramidal spire. The transitions between the various sections are masked by the little ancillary towers.

The spire is 91 m (298 ft) high and is crowned by a 5 m (16 ft) high gilded copper weather-vane representing the Archangel Michael wrought in 1454 by the coppersmith Martin van Rode. The portal is not in the centre of the tower. It is said that when the architect realised his mistake he threw himself off the top of the tower but what he had in fact done was to retain the foundations and portal of the former Belfried and extend its right-hand wall so that he kept enough of the foundations to build the new tower.

The sculptures in the porch are 15th c. and are attributed to Claus Sulter. They are thought to have decorated the entrance of the demolished Belfried. The door itself dates from the late 16th or early 17th c.

The heart of Brussels: Grand'Place with Town Hall ▶

Town Hall

Courtyard and rear wings

The two fountains in the courtyard represent the Scheldt (right), by Pierre-Denis Plumiers (1715), and the Maas, by Jan de Kinder (1714) after J.-A. Anneessens.
The wings are in the Louis XIV style (Corneille van Nerven, 1708–17). This was the site of the Cloth Hall in medieval times.

Interior

Ground-floor vestibule: "The Beheading of St Paul", drawing by Bernard van Orley (1491–1542) and tapestry based on this drawing (17th c.).
Maximilian Hall: tapestries depicting the life of Clovis by Venderborght and based on drawings attributed to Charles Lebrun.
Galerie Grangé (1718): portraits of rulers, by Louis Grangé (1686–1764).
Mayor's antechamber: pictures of old Brussels by J.-B. van Moor (1819–84).
Ceremonial staircase: busts of all the Mayors since 1830. Murals of the history of Brussels by Jacques Lalaing (1893).
Gothic Hall: The rulers were enthroned here under the former régime. The last enthronement was that of King William I of the Netherlands on 21 September 1815.
This hall used to be decorated with paintings by Rogier van der Weyden but they fell victim to the bombardment of 1695.
In 1868 it was renovated by Ch. Jamar in the Neo-Gothic style and contains Mechelen tapestries depicting the Brussels guilds, made by Bracquerie (1877–80) after drawings by G. Geets, and gilded bronze statues of former rulers of the city.
Registry Office: allegorical paintings by Cardon (1881). Ceiling with coats of arms of the guilds.

The Maximilian Hall in the Town Hall

Maison du Roi (Broodhuis) – Municipal Museum

The Maison du Roi (House of the King), after the Town Hall the
finest building in the market place and directly opposite the
Town Hall, is so-called not because a king once lived here, as
one might suppose, but because it used to house the law court
where justice was dispensed in the name of the King of Spain.
Today the Maison du Roi houses Brussels' Municipal Museum
(Musée communal) with rich collections dealing with the
hitory of the city, and including the costumes of the Manneken-
Pis, etc.

In the early 13th c. the building that stood here was known as
the Broodhuis (bread house) but by the 15th c. it was only
being used by bakers from outside Brussels as a place to
market their wares. The Broodhuis later came to be called
't Hertogenhuis (Duke's House) because it had once housed
ducal law courts.

History of the building

The building was demolished in 1512–13 but rebuilding began
as early as 1515, this time on piles because of the marshy site,
and involved the greatest architects of the time – Anton
Keldermans, Ludwig van Bodeghem and Heinrich van Prede.
When Philip II added more law courts the name of the house
changed for a third time and became Pretorium Regium, or
House of the King in the vernacular.
In the 17th c. the Infanta Isabella had the house rebuilt in stone
and dedicated it to the Holy Virgin, whose stone statue was
placed on the façade.
In 1695 the building was almost completely destroyed by
Marshal Villeroy's bombardment and for over half a century the
ruined Maison du Roi cast a sombre shadow over the market
place.
In 1768 it was decided that it should be rebuilt, but this was
done with no thought for its traditional architecture: the steps
disappeared and were replaced by an ordinary staircase at
ground level; the side walls were filled in without any
ornamentation; the roof was replaced by an ordinary one and
lost its graceful gables, statues, merlons and small towers. Later
parts of the façade were even plastered over and whitewashed.
Needless to say, the whole effect was hideous.
During the French occupation the house was declared public
property and renamed (not surprisingly) the House of the
People.
The city sold this building to the Marquis Paul Arconati
Visconti, who in turn sold it to Simon Pick. In 1860 the city of
Brussels bought it back from Simon Pick's daughter, who was
the wife of the painter Ludwig Gallait.
It was decided to pull it down and have it rebuilt in accordance
with the original plans. This hard task was entrusted to the City
Architect Victor Jamar, who went on to create a true
masterpiece in terms of his architectural skill and patience.
Its reconstruction took longer that it had originally taken to
build. Begun in 1873, building work was not completed until
22 years later. Victor Jamar consulted the old engravings and,
with his fellow architect Beyaert, successfully re-created this
fine building.

The façade, sides, arcades and cornices are of bluestone (a
blue-grey sandstone), decorated with a lattice-work of white
stone from Gobertange; both types of stone come from Belgian
quarries.

Exterior

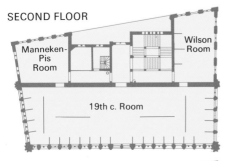

SECOND FLOOR

Manneken-Pis Room

Wilson Room

19th c. Room

FIRST FLOOR

Office

Office

Ceramics Room

GROUND FLOOR

Rue du Poivre

1

Con-cierge

6

Rue des Harengs

Rue Chair et Pain

2

3

4

5

En-trance

Grand'Place

Maison du Roi
Broodhuis

Musée Communal
Municipal Museum

DEUXIEME ETAGE
TWEEDE VERDIEP
SECOND FLOOR

PREMIER ETAGE
EERSTE VERDIEP
FIRST FLOOR

REZ-DE-CHAUSSEE
GELIJKVLOERS
GROUND FLOOR

1 Guilds Room
2 St Michael Room
3 Prophet Room
4 Retable Room
5 Meleagros Room
6 Caryatid Room

10m
33ft

The ground-floor arcade consists of nine arches each resting on two free-standing columns. The first-floor arcades are supported by clusters of columns. The vaulting is of brick with bands of white stone.

Statues

The statues in the central archway represent: Marie of Burgundy (she bequeathed the Maison du Roi to the city in 1477), Charles V (he ordered it to be rebuilt), John I the Victorious, and Henry I (he gave Brussels its first charter in 1229).
The statuettes that decorate the façade, the attic windows and the gables and the coats of arms are of gilded cuprite: two heraldic lions holding a coat of arms; four lions bearing a

banner (by A. Desenfans); a crossbowman and a longbowman, Dillens' armed heralds; a cook, a pun on the nickname Kiekenfretters (chicken-guzzlers) – the people of Brussels have been called this since time immemorial – and four figures representing the military guilds of Brussels.

The spire of the tower is of slate-clad oak and its lucarns are decorated with wrought-iron spikes. The crown and the bread in the wrought-iron weather-vane symbolise the two names, Broodhuis and Maison du Roi.

Tower

In June 1895 the tower was given a 16-bell carillon by the bell-founder Jef Denijn, the heaviest of which had a diameter of over 1 m (3 ft 3 in) and weighed 600 kg (11·8 cwt), while a second peal of 24 bells was hung on the second floor of the campanile. This carillon was subsequently taken down, as were all Brussels' carillons, because they supposedly disturbed the sleep of the inhabitants. The Bruxellois had the unpleasant memory, in any case, of the huge carillon that, because of its weight, had caused the collapse of the municipal belfry alongside the Church of St Nicholas.

Many a famous execution took place in front of the Maison du Roi, including those of Egmont and Hoorn who had been sentenced to death by the Duke of Alba's "Council of Blood". On 5 June 1568, the eve of his execution, Count Egmont was brought to the Maison du Roi, where he spent the night in a room on the second floor.

Place of execution

Long afterwards a memorial commemorating the shameful execution of the two much-loved noblemen was erected on the exact spot in front of the steps of the Maison du Roi where they

In summer one can take coffee outside the Maison du Roi

had been so infamously beheaded. This memorial by Fraikin and its fountain were later moved to the Place du Petit Sablon. Anneessens, the Brussels People's Tribune, was also executed on the same spot after the Marquis de Prié had sentenced him to death.

Municipal Museum

Work was begun on setting up the Municipal Museum (Musée communal) over half a century ago in the building that had previously housed the city council offices.

Ground floor:

Immediately to the left of the ground-floor entrance are 14th and 15th c. sculptures. The adjoining room contains sculptures of the 16th–18th c. The finest of these are those by J. Duquesnoy the Elder. Pottery and pewter of the 17th–19th c. are on display in the former Guilds Room.

To the right of the entrance is a room of 15th and 16th c. paintings by the Brussels school. The incomparably fine altar-paintings created during the heyday of artistic achievement in Brussels are especially noteworthy. In the adjoining room are tapestries of the 16th–18th c. These exhibits afford only a brief glimpse of that period's vast artistic output. On display in the former Caryatid Room are unique items of porcelain and exceptionally fine silverwork of the 18th and 19th c.

First floor:

This floor charts the development of the city of Brussels by illustrating its urban growth in terms of settlement, roads and transport, open spaces, imposing buildings and housing.

Second floor:

The displays on this floor show particular aspects of the city's history in greater detail: political institutions, commerce, society, religion, culture, handicrafts, Brussels as a capital. Here the biggest attraction is, of course, the room full of the costumes of the Manneken-Pis (see entry).

The museum gets plenty of foreign visitors but, unfortunately, is not so much frequented by the Bruxellois themselves, although it is well worth a visit.

Guild houses in the Grand'Place

The first houses in the Grand'Place were built of wood. These were all destroyed, together with another 4000 in the city, during the 36-hour bombardment of Brussels on 13 and 15 August 1695 by Marshal de Villeroy, acting on the orders of Louis XIV of France.

The present-day stone houses went up almost as soon as the rubble was cleared. Built mostly by rich and powerful guilds, each house is still called by a name recalling its original purpose.

The houses were all built between 1696 and 1700 in an Italian Baroque style somewhat modified by their Flemish architects. When looking at these houses it should be remembered that architects in the 17th c. were primarily painters, sculptors, wood-carvers or stonemasons and that their style of building was bound to be influenced by their basic calling.

Le Roi d'Espagne (Nos. 1–2)

The first house on the west side, to the right of the Town Hall, numbered 1 and 2, is the House of the Bakers, known chiefly as Le Roi d' Espagne (the King of Spain).

It is in the classical Italian style and encompasses the three orders of columns: Doric on the ground floor, Ionic on the first floor and Corinthian on the second floor.

A comparison with the Bellone House in the Rue de Flandres

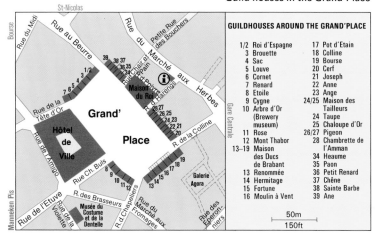

GUILDHOUSES AROUND THE GRAND'PLACE

1/2	Roi d'Espagne	17	Pot d'Etain
3	Brouette	18	Colline
4	Sac	19	Bourse
5	Louve	20	Cerf
6	Cornet	21	Joseph
7	Renard	22	Anne
8	Etoile	23	Ange
9	Cygne	24/25	Maison des
10	Arbre d'Or		Tailleurs
	(Brewery	24	Taupe
	museum)	25	Chaloupe d'Or
11	Rose	26/27	Pigeon
12	Mont Thabor	28	Chambrette de
13–19	Maison		l'Amman
	des Ducs	34	Heaume
	de Brabant	35	Paon
13	Renommée	36	Petit Renard
14	Hermitage	37	Chêne
15	Fortune	38	Sainte Barbe
16	Moulin à Vent	39	Ane

50m
150ft

seems to indicate that both were the work of the same architect, the sculptor Jean Cosyn. Above the vaulted door is a bust of Bishop Aubert, the patron saint of bakers. The inscription reads, 'During his lifetime this saint was notable for his admirable works of charity to the poor'.

At first-floor level the wall is decorated with medallions of the Roman Emperors Marcus Aurelius, Nerva, Decius and Trajan. At second-floor level a bust of Charles II is surrounded by trophies and two prisoners in chains, with, written on the base, 'King of Spain'.

Above the second floor is a balustrade with six statues: Power, Corn, Wind, Fire, Water and Foresight.

The house is crowned with an octagonal dome topped by a golden statue of Fame.

The interior is a popular old inn and beer-cellar, Au Roi d'Espagne.

Number 3 is the House of the Tallow-Makers' Guild also known as La Brouette (The Wheelbarrow). Built in the Italian-Flemish style, like the Roi d'Espagne it, too, has the three orders of columns. Although it is not known who the architect was, the sculptor Jean Cosyn is known to have worked on it.

La Brouette (No. 3)

The façade between ground floor and first floor is decorated with tablets inscribed "The House of the Tallowmakers" and "The Wheelbarrow". The tablets between the first and second floors give the year the house was built: "Anno 1697".

The Corinthian columns on the third floor are surmounted by a gable with, in the niche, a statue of Saint Giles, patron saint of tallowmakers.

The house at No. 4, Le Sac (The Bag), is the House of the Joiners and Coopers. The architect is not known, but it is known to have been rebuilt by the joiner Pastorana.

Le Sac (No. 4)

The house is in two parts: the lower part, built in 1644 in the Classical style, escaped the conflagration of 1695 and was restored by Pastorana; the upper part is largely Pastorana's handiwork.

Guild houses in the Grand'Place

The statue above the main door is of a man holding a bag into which another man is putting his hands.

La Louve (No. 5)

The house at No. 5 got its name, La Louve (The She-Wolf), from the bas-relief over the door showing Romulus and Remus being suckled by the she-wolf.

This house was only partially destroyed in 1695, rebuilt to the original plans in the Flemish-Italian style and acquired by the Guild of Archers.

At first-floor level, between the triglyphs and the cornices, are various articles relating to archery. The balcony is decorated with a lyre and a quiver.

At second-floor level there is a statue in front of each Corinthian column and underneath is written, from left to right, "Truth here", "Falsehood there", "Let there be Peace", "Away with Discord".

Truth, who holds an open book in her hand, has a crouching eagle by her side. Falsehood holds a mask and is accompanied by a fox. Peace bears a sheaf and is surrounded by doves. Discord brandishes a firebrand, with wolves standing at her feet. The inscriptions read, above Truth, "The mainstay of the Empire"; above Falsehood, "The pitfall of the State"; above Peace, "The saving of Mankind" and above Discord, "The ruin of the Republic!".

At third-floor level the columns are decorated with medallions of Trajan, Tiberius, Augustus and Julius Caesar. Between Truth and the Trajan medallion a sun lights up the world. On the adjoining buttress a birdcage and a net depict cunning. Between the medallion of Augustus and Peace is a globe to which the Emperor is bringing universal peace. On the last buttress a bleeding heart and two crossed firebrands depict civil war.

In the triangular gable above the third floor is a bas-relief showing Apollo seizing the Python. On the gable stands a phoenix with the inscription "Burnt, I arose more proudly by the grace of the Guild of Sebastian".

Le Cornet (No. 6)

The first house at No. 6 was named Le Cornet (The Horn of Plenty) in 1434 by the Guild of Boatmen. The building was destroyed in 1695 and replaced in 1697 by the present house, built in the Flemish-Italian style by the joiner Pastorana, who, since it was the House of the Boatmen, shaped the gable to represent the poop-deck of a galleon.

At the mezzanine level a bas-relief depicts a horn of plenty. At first-floor level each column is crowned by a golden vase of flowers, while on the second floor the windows are each surmounted by an oval arcade, with the columns being replaced by parts of a ship. Above this floor a giant newt between two seahorses can be seen catching a fish. The poop-deck gable carries a medallion of Charles II of Spain, topped by two lions guarding the coat of arms.

Le Renard (No. 7)

The house next door at No. 7 is known as Le Renard (The Fox), because of the golden fox over the doorway, and belonged to the Guild of Haberdashers.

The building style mingles the three orders of columns and Baroque fantasy with elements of Louis XIV.

At the mezzanine level are four bas-reliefs: children handling skins, draper's shop, a dye shop and a china shop.

The façade at first-floor level is decorated by five statues. The one in the centre represents Justice – she is blindfolded and has a sword in one hand and scales in the other. The other four statues symbolise Europe, Asia, Africa and America.

There are four caryatides on the floor above, the first carrying the Golden Fleece, the second holding ears of corn, the third grapes and the fourth flowers. The statue at the very top is of St Nicholas, patron saint of haberdashers.

The first house on the south side of the square, to the left of the Town Hall, known as L'Etoile (The Star), is the smallest as well as one of the oldest houses in the Grand'Place. Used by the City Bailiff as an office as early as the 13th c., it was destroyed in 1695 and later rebuilt, only to be demolished again in 1852 when the street was widened. It was finally rebuilt in 1897 over a colonnade.

It is simple in style – four pillars support the gable which is crowned by a star.

In 1356 it was on this house that Louis de Maele, Count of Flanders, raised his banner after conquering the Grand Duchy of Brabant. It was torn down a few months later by the folk-hero of Brussels, Everard 't Serclaes, when his small band of partisans had liberated the city. Shortly afterwards the Duke of Brabant returned to Brussels in triumph but 't Serclaes had been captured and tortured by the Count of Gaasbeek. He was found dying by a priest who brought him to the Star, where at that time the Duke's Justice of the Peace resided. The angry Bruxellois then stormed the Castle of Gaasbeek and burnt it to the ground.

The monument to 't Serclaes is under the colonnade of L'Etoile, on the corner of Charles-Buls Street. The arm of his statue is polished bright from having been rubbed by the Bruxellois since, traditionally, their wishes will then come true. The scenes on the plaques above are 't Serclaes with his partisans, the Duke of Brabant re-entering Brussels, and the burning of Gaasbeek Castle.

Le Cygne (No. 9 – The Swan), next to L'Etoile, was rebuilt in 1698 by a private citizen after the 1695 bombardment and became in 1720 the Guild House of the Butchers.

The style is no longer that of Flemish Baroque, but is already that of the 18th c., influenced by Louis XIV.

A swan, its wings outspread, stands above the door. The first-floor balcony was a novelty in its day. The three statues above the second floor, added in 1904, represent Plenty, Agriculture and the Butchery Trade.

Number 10, L'Arbre d'Or (The Golden Tree), was destroyed in 1695 and rebuilt by the brewers, who had bought it from the carpet-weavers. Its architect, Guillaume de Bruyn, seems here to have first introduced the free-standing column into Brussels. The ground floor and upper floors are reminiscent of Italian Classicism while the circular gable has retained the Flemish style. The statue on the plinth of Charles of Lorraine replaced, in 1752, a statue of Prince Maximilian II Immanuel of Bavaria, who had been Governor-General of the Netherlands at the time of the French bombardment. Between the storeys three bas-reliefs depict the grape harvest, carting beet and the hop harvest. Nowadays L'Arbre d'Or houses the brewery museum.

L'Etoile (No. 8)

Le Cygne (No. 9)

L'Arbre d'Or (No. 10)

59

Guild houses in the Grand'Place

Guild Houses: Le Roi d'Espagne

La Brouette

Le Sac

and La Louve

The house at No. 11, La Rose (The Rose), is in the 17th c. Flemish style with the three orders of columns. The façade has been kept very plain, in the unpretentious style of the late 17th c.

La Rose (No. 11)

The former Mont Thabor is today called Aux Trois Couleurs (The three Colours). Like the Rose, it is built in the simple bourgeois style.

Le Mont Thabor (No. 12)

La Maison des Ducs de Brabant (The House of the Dukes of Brabant) is actually a group of six houses with one single façade. Number 13, the first house on the east side of the square, is Fame, followed by The Hermitage (No. 14), Fortune (No. 15), The Windmill (No. 16), The Pewter Pot (No. 17), The Hill (No. 18) and La Bourse (The Stock Exchange) (No. 19). Following the 1695 bombardment these houses were rebuilt in 1698 in the Flemish-Italian style by the architect Guillaume de Bruyn.
The façade is in two sections, with the lower section taking in the mezzanine and ground floor and the busts of the Dukes of Brabant on the capitals of the 19 Ionic columns.
The shields above the door depict the Hermitage, Fortune, the Pewter Pot and the Hill, while those below the windows of the first floor are of the Windmill and La Bourse.
The upper section is embellished with Corinthian columns, while the second-floor pillars are decorated with tools symbolising the guilds.
Two bas-reliefs on the second floor of The Hill depict the Imperial Eagle of Austria.
The Windmill was the home of the French writer Victor Hugo for a few months in 1852.

La Maison des Ducs de Brabant (Nos. 13–19)

The first three houses on the north side of the Grand'Place are much simpler and more sober in style than the others in the square. The first one, on the corner, owes its name, Le Cerf, to the deer above the door.
The next two, which share a common façade and are known as Joseph and Anne, are simple 17th c. town houses.

Le Cerf; Joseph et Anne (Nos. 20–22)

L'Ange (The Angel – No. 23) was built in the Flemish-Italian style, with Ionic columns in the lower section and Corinthian in the upper section, the gable being supported by two Corinthian columns.

L'Ange (No. 23)

Numbers 24 and 25 were originally two houses, La Taupe (The Mole) and La Chaloupe d'Or (The Golden Sloop). They belonged to the Tailors' Guild and were rebuilt in the Flemish-Italian style after 1695 by Guillaume de Bruyn, who gave them a single façade and used the same design for L'Arbre d'Or (see above). As in L'Ange, the lower columns are Ionic and the upper ones Corinthian. Above the Corinthian columns is an ornamented cornice and above that a triangular gable. The middle window on the first floor is also crowned by a triangular gable, while the gable above the other two windows is vaulted. The bust over the door is of St Barbe, patron saint of tailors, while the statue on top of the house is of St Boniface.

La Maison des Tailleurs (Nos. 24–25)

Le Pigeon (The Dove – Nos. 26–27) was the House of the Painters. Simple and Classical in style, it leaves no scope for

Le Pigeon (Nos. 26–27)

Flemish flights of fancy. The columns are Doric on the ground floor, Ionic on the first floor and Corinthian on the second.

La Chambrette de L'Amman

La Chambrette de l'Amman, the House of the Amman, the Duke's representative on the medieval town council, is nowadays known as the Arms of Brabant because of the Duke's coat of arms on the façade. Like Le Pigeon, it was built in the simple Classical style based on the three orders of columns.

La Maison du Roi

La Maison du Roi (see above) is the second most important building in the Grand'Place.

Le Heaume (No. 34)

Since the 15th c. No. 34 has been called Le Heaume (The Helmet). The three orders of columns have been used here, too, while the roof gable is in the Flemish style.

Nos. 35–39

The neighbouring houses recall the old Brussels houses that lack any trace of Classicism – The Peacock (No. 35), The Foxcub (No. 36), The Oak (No. 37), St Barbe (No. 38) and The Donkey (No. 39).

Grimbergen

Location
12 km (8 miles) N of the city centre

Bus
G

The village of Grimbergen on the northern outskirts of Brussels is where an abbey, once very rich, was founded in the 12th c. The stately monastery church (1660–1700) is one of the finest Baroque buildings in Belgium.
The Mira Observatory is at 20 Abdijstraat and interesting guided tours can be organised on request (tel. 269 1280).

*Halle (Hal)

Location
15 km (9 miles) SW of Brussels

The Flemish town of Halle (or Hal in French) lies on the River Senne and the canal linking Brussels and Charleroi, not far from the Flemish-Walloon language frontier, and has an industrial base of iron, textiles, leather and foodstuffs.

St-Martinus Basiliek

The principal feature of the townscape is St-Martinus Basiliek (Basilica of Our Lady), a notable building in Brabant-Gothic style (14th–15th c.), its elegant architecture also betraying a French influence. It has some remarkable sculptures, the oldest of which (14th c.) are on the west portal and the tower, and in the choir (especially the row of Apostles over the arches, apparently contemporary with and in the style of Klaus Sluter), while the rather later ones are on the south portal and in the chapel north of the choir, which has a fine alabaster altar by J. Mone (1533; a Renaissance work with reliefs of the Seven Sacraments and statuettes) and the marble memorial to the Dauphin Jacques (d. 1460), son of Louis XI of France. Above the modern High Altar is the wooden statuette of the Virgin, believed to work miracles and known to have been in Halle since the 13th c. The bell-tower houses a museum which includes bells dating from the time of Charles V.

Town Hall

The Stadhuis (Town Hall) in the Grote Markt (market place) is a picturesque ornate brick building built in 1616.

Heysel A2/8

The plateau of Heysel, in the north of Brussels near the Royal
Park of Laeken (see entry), was laid out several decades ago
with sporting facilities and exhibition sites amidst its broad
expanse of lawns and woodland. Its most prominent landmark
is the Atomium (see entry) built in 1958 for the World Fair.

Location
N of Brussels

Metro station
Heysel

At the top of the Boulevard du Centenaire is the Palais du
Centenaire, a multi-tiered exhibition centre built in the 1930s.
Its middle section is 31 m (102 ft) high and has concrete
merlons decorated with four huge statues by E. Rombaux.

Palais du Centenaire

The Brussels International Trade Mart, next to the Palais du
Centenaire, was built between 1973 and 1975 and is the work
of John Portman, the famous American architect.

Brussels International Trade
Mart

West of the Boulevard du Centenaire is the large sports
complex centred on Heysel Stadium (Stade du Heysel or Stade
du Centenaire). The stadium, which holds 71,000 spectators,
was built in 1930 with Van Neck as its architect.

Heysel Stadium

The new Planetarium (1973) of which Aerts was the architect,
stands just south of Heysel Stadium and has a dome 24 m
(79 ft) in diameter.
Farther to the west is the interesting Cité Modèle.

Planetarium

Hôtel Ravenstein C4

The 14th c. Hôtel Ravenstein stands at the top of the Rue
Ravenstein (see Mont des Arts), where Brussels had its Jewish
Quarter in the Middle Ages. It is the last surviving large building
in Brussels from the Burgundian period and has recently been
lovingly restored. Its central courtyard and the so-called Jews'
Staircase are especially picturesque.

Location
Rue Ravenstein

Metro station
Gare Centrale

Ixelles D3-5

The suburb of Ixelles south of the outer ring road (Boulevards
Extérieurs) has as its main artery the busy Chaussée d'Ixelles,
with three shopping arcades leading off its upper part. The
Church of Saint Boniface in the centre of Ixelles was rebuilt in
the Neo-Gothic style in the middle of the last century.

Location
S of Brussels

Metro station
Porte de Namur, Place
Louise

The Musée Communal in the Rue Jean van Volsem has
interesting work by more modern, mostly Belgian artists, the
Belgian Impressionists in particular.

Musée Communal

The Chaussée d'Ixelles descends past the Town Hall to Bas-
Ixelles, with its pretty lakes, the Etangs d'Ixelles, and the tall
buildings of Belgian Radio and Television.

Etangs d'Ixelles

The peaceful cemetery at Ixelles contains the grave of the poet
Charles de Coster (1827–79) who is principally remembered
for his "Till Eulenspiegel".

Cemetery

Laeken

See Château Royal de Laeken
See Notre-Dame de Laeken

*Maison d'Erasme (Erasmus's House)

Location
31 Rue du Chapitre
B-1070 Anderlecht

Tram
103

Buses
46, 49, 76

Opening times
10–midday and 2–5 p.m.

Closed
Tues. and Fri.

The Maison d'Erasme (Erasmus's house), in the suburb of
Anderlecht in the south-west of Brussels and near the
Collegiate Church of Sts-Pierre et Guidon (see entry), is the
delightful early 16th c. building where Erasmus of Rotterdam,
the famous humanist (1466–1536), resided in 1521.
The interior is laid out as a museum. Apart from fine period
furniture and wall-hangings, it contains a collection of
documents illustrating the life of the author of "In Praise of
Folly" ("Laus Stultitiae"). There are letters written by the great
scholar, first editions of his works, a letter from Charles V,
paintings and sketches (including some by Holbein and
Dürer), archaeological finds from Anderlecht, etc.
Illustration on p. 67.

*Manneken-Pis   C3

Location
Rue de l'Etuve, on the corner
of Rue du Chêne

Metro station
Gare Centrale

Only a few hundred yards from the Grand'Place (see entry), in
the busy Rue de l'Etuve, is what must be the most famous of
Brussels' monuments and "its oldest citizen" – the Manneken-
Pis, the bronze statue of a little boy blithely peeing away into
the ancient fountain. This popular little figure has had a
turbulent history: he has been stolen several times since he was
first fashioned in 1619 by Jérôme Duquesnoy the Elder, who
had been commissioned by the City Fathers to replace an earlier

The best-known sight in Brussels – Manneken-Pis

similar version. After the last theft, in 1817, he was recovered in pieces and recast in bronze. The original base and two small basins made by the stonemason Daniel Raessens in 1619 were replaced in 1770 by a niche of bluestone.

The Manneken-Pis wears clothes on special occasions and his wardrobe includes about 300 costumes that have been given him from all over the world. He is said to have acquired his first suit of clothes – Bavarian-blue national dress – in 1698 from Maximilian Emanuel, the Bavarian Prince at that time Governor-General of the Netherlands. When French grenadiers were caught trying to steal him in 1747, King Louis XV of France presented him, as compensation, with a gold-embroidered brocade suit, his second costume, and made him a Knight of the Order of St Louis. Nowadays his collection of costumes is on display in the Maison du Roi in the Grand'Place (see entry).

The Manneken-Pis has many legends surrounding his origins. According to one of them, when duke Godefroy III was taken by his father, Godefroy II, at the age of a few months to spur on the soldiers at the Battle of Reinsbeke, he raised himself up in his cradle at the decisive moment of the battle and "spent a penny", this being the act immortalised in the fountain in the Rue de l'Etuve. Another story has it that this is what the 5-year-old youngest son of a Count d'Hove was found doing during a procession in honour of the Blessed Sacrament in Brussels at the time of the First Crusade. Yet another of the many curious tales is that a wicked fairy is supposed to have caught a lad in the act of "watering" her stairs, so she cast a spell on him, condemning him to do it forever and he turned into a stone statue.

Les Marolles (district of the city)   D3

Les Marolles is the old working-class quarter centred around the Rue Haute and the Rue Blaes and their maze of little alleyways. Above it towers the gigantic bulk of the Palais de Justice. This quarter revolves around the Church of Notre-Dame de la Chapelle (see entry) and the Place du Jeu de Balle, Brussels' Petticoat Lane with its Flea Market (see entry).

The quarter owes its name to a former Convent of the Apostolic Sisters of Maricolles. The Bovendael quarter between the Rue l'Epée, the Rue de l'Evential and the Rue Haute was the old red light district and was cordoned off from the rest of the Marolles in 1597 to prevent the "girls" coming into contact with the other people living in the quarter. The situation changed in the early 17th c. when this part was settled by a religious community known as Les Minimés.

The inhabitants of Les Marolles are renowned for their colourful, Cockney-like sense of humour (See Toone's Puppet Theatre, Marolle dialect) and, like London's Eastenders, they tend to be low-waged manual workers, junk-dealers and market traders. With their typical independence and sense of "bloody-mindedness" they have set up their own "Free Commune" which organises the Bruegel festival every year (see Practical Information – Calendar of Events) in honour of Pieter Bruegel who lived and was buried in their district (see Maison Bruegel and Notre-Dame de la Chapelle).

Location
Around the Rue Haute and the Rue Blaes, below the Palais de Justice

Buses
20 21, 34, 38, 71, 95, 96

Trams
92, 93, 94

Metro Art

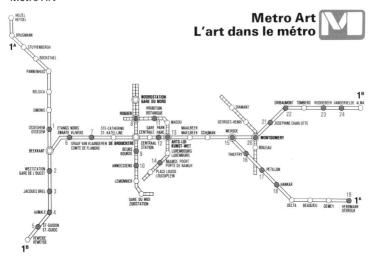

NUMBER on the plan	STATION name in French/ Dutch	WORK OF ART *Name (type, year)*	ARTIST Name
● 1	Osseghem/Ossegem	*Stop the run!* (copper relief; 1982) *Driehoek in beweging* (marble sculpture; 1980)	Reinhoud (D'Haese) Hild Van Sumere
● 2	Gare de l'Ouest/Weststation	*Compositie* (glass painting; 1982)	Guy Vandenbranden
● 3	Jacques Brel	*Coming up for air* (acrylic painting; 1982)	Maurice Wyckaert
● 4	Aumale	*Metrorama 78* (photographic mural; 1982)	Jean-Paul Laenen
● 5	St-Guidon/St-Guido	*Wij leven* (metal mural relief; 1978)	Frans Minnaert
● 6	Etangs Noirs/Zwarte Vijvers	*De Zwarte Vijvers* (mural in oils; 1980)	Jan Burssens
● 7	Comte de Flandre/Graaf van Vlaanderen	*16 × Icarus* (ceiling relief; 1978)	Paul Van Hoeydonck
● 8	Rogier	*The Fall of Troy* (mural in oils; 1978)	Jan Cox
● 9	Bourse/Beurs	*Moving Ceiling* (steel cylinder; 1976) *Nos vieux trams bruxellois* (oil painting; 1978)	Pol Bury Paul Delvaux
● 10	Anneessens	*Sept écritures* (word-painting; 1976)	Pierre Aléchinsky und Christian Dotremont
● 11	Botanique/Kruidtuin	*Les Voyageurs* (21 coloured wooden figures; 1979) *The Last Migration* (copper sculpture; 1977) *Tramification fluide – Tramification syncopée* (coloured steel tubes; 1978)	Pierre Caille Jean-Pierre Ghysels Emile Souply
● 12	Parc/Park	*La ville* (wall mosaic; 1972) *Happy metro to you* (coloured wooden figures; 1972)	Roger Dudant Marc Mendelson
● 13	Arts-Loi/Kunst-Wet	*Isjtar* (lacquered wooden reliefs; 1976) *Ortem* (coloured ceramic tiles; 1976)	Gilbert Decock Jean Rets
● 14	Porte de Namur/Naamse Poort	*Het uiteindelijk verkeer* (four round enamelled ceramic reliefs; 1979)	Octave Landuyt
● 15	Mérode	*Carrelage cinq* (coloured ceramic tiles; 1976) *Ensor: "Vive la Sociale (?)"* (oil painting; 1976)	Jean Gilbert Roger Raveel
● 16	Thieffry	*Aequus Nox* (tinted mirror glass; 1976) *Sculptures* (bronze and steel; 1976)	Vic Gentils Felix Roulin
● 17	Pétillon	*Que la mer épargne* (aluminium chrome relief; 1976)	Lismonde
● 18	Hankar	*Notre temps* (acrylic painting on concrete; 1976)	Roer Somville
● 19	Herrmann Debroux	*L'aviateur* (bronze sculpture; 1967) *Ode aan een bergrivier* (bronze; 1982)	Roel D'Haese Rik Poot
● 20	Montgomery	*Rythme mondial* (coloured ceramic tiles; 1975) *Magic City* (mural in oils; 1975) *Thema's* (six oil-paintings; 1975)	Jo Delahaut Jean-Michel Folon Pol Mara
● 21	Joséphine-Charlotte	*La fleur unique ou les oiseaux émerveillés* (coloured wooden reliefs; 1979)	Serge Vandercam
● 22	Gribaumont	*Le Tropolitain* (mural in oils; 1976)	Frans Nellens
● 23	Roodebeek	*Intégration bruxelloise* (steel and glass; 1981)	Luc Peire
● 24	Vandervelde	*La grande taupe et le petit peintre* (huge mural in acrylic paints; 1981)	Paul de Gobert

Art in the Metro

Erasmus's House

*Metro Art (L'art dans le Métro)

Since work began on the Brussels Underground in 1965 the architects responsible for the stations have been thinking about how to make them original. They started with the idea of getting some pleasing decoration on the walls then set about getting the artists to do the work. There have been some very remarkable works produced so far, such as enamelled wall tiles, acrylic paintings on concrete, silk-screen prints on glass, reliefs made of various materials, marble pieces, mosaics and a range of bronze, steel and wood sculptures.

Musée de la Dynastie

See Palais Royal

Musée de la Gueuze (Gueuze Beer Museum)   D2

North of the Gare du Midi, in the Rue Gheude, is the Gueuze Museum (Musée Bruxellois de la Gueuze), one of the most unusual museums in the city. It is housed in the only brewery in Brussels where Gueuze beer is still brewed in the traditional way (Brasserie Cantillon).

Location
56 Rue Gheude

Buses
20, 46, 62

67

Musée du Cinéma

Opening times
18 Oct.–30 Apr. only Sat.
10 a.m.–5 p.m. or by
arrangement

Gueuze beer, a speciality of the Brussels area and a blend of Lambic, is brewed by a process of spontaneous fermentation using about one-third raw wheat, two-thirds malted barley and 3 year-old hops. The individual stages in the brewing process can be followed in the museum.

Lambic

Lambic is one of the so-called "wild" beers, i.e. fermentation is not brought about by the addition of yeast in the fermenting vat but begins spontaneously in barrels containing special strains of yeast (*Brettanomyces lambicus* and *brucelensis*). The Lambic is produced after two to three days of fermentation but then has to be stored in the barrel for several years. The actual Gueuze is obtained by blending several types of Lambic and is then bottled and, like champagne, sealed with corks and wire.

This is followed by fermentation within the bottle and a maturing process lasting about two years. Gueuze beer is rather dark, not very gassy and slightly sour in taste. It should be drunk at cellar temperature (7–10 °C) and, if it has not been filtered, care should be taken to see that the lees stay in the bottle.

Musée du Cinéma (film museum)

See Palais des Beaux-Arts

---

*Musée Instrumental (Royal Conservatoire collection of musical instruments)   D3

Location
Main Building: 17 Place du Petit Sablon
Annexe: 37 Place du Grand Sablon

Buses
20, 21, 34, 95, 96

Trams
92, 94

Opening times
Main Building: Tues., Thurs., Sat. 2.30–4.30 p.m., Wed. 5–7 p.m., Sun. 10.30 a.m.–12.30 p.m.
Annexe: Tues., Sat. 4–6 p.m., Wed. 5–7 p.m., Sun. 10.30 a.m.–12.30 p.m.

This very interesting museum, founded in 1928, is housed in the Royal Music Conservatoire (Conservatoire Royal de Musique), which was built in 1876–77 to plans by the architect J.-P. Cluysenaer on the site of the former Hôtel Tour et Tassis (demolished in 1872), which had been the residence of the family of the same name (chapel and family vault in Notre-Dame du Sablon, see entry). It was not far from here that François de Tour et Tassis organised the first international postal service in 1516 (commemorative plaque). Together with the Annexe (different opening times!) in the Grand Sablon (see entry) it houses the largest and most important collection of musical instruments in the world, from almost every country and every age. The oldest of the over 5000 items dates from the Bronze Age; 150 instruments are unique and the collection ranges versatilely from primitive Indian flutes to everything required for a full brass band.

Exhibits particularly worth seeing include:

Viola da gamba by the famous instrument-maker Gaspard l'Effoprugcar (16th c.) entitled "au plan de la ville de Paris".

Spinet by Antonius Patavinus (1550), richly decorated, bearing the coat of arms of the Bembos, a noble Venetian family.

Componium by Nikolaus Winkel (1821) which, once set in motion, produces endless variations on a given theme.

Harpsichords (spinets) by Rückers & Sons (16th–17th c.), the famous Antwerp family of keyboard-makers.

The collection of instruments belonging to Adolphe Sax, inventor of the saxophone, can be seen in the Annexe.

The museum also has an extensive music library and a photographic collection. Visitors can also listen to recordings of old instruments.

Library, photographs

Evening concerts and music recitals on old instruments are often staged in the Annexe (details in the daily papers; tel. 5 11 35 95).

Events

The Conservatoire's fine concert hall (entrance 30 Rue Royale; tel. 5 11 04 27) serves as the venue for the early rounds of the world-famous Concours Musical Reine Elisabeth (Queen Elisabeth Music Competition; see Facts and Figures – Culture). The final rounds take place in the Palais des Beaux-Arts.

Concert hall

*Musée Royal de l'Afrique Centrale (Central Africa Museum)

The Musée Royal de l'Afrique Centrale (Central Africa Museum) is one of the most interesting museums in Belgium. Only a few miles outside the city centre, it is located in Tervuren and is reached by taking the broad, tree-lined Avenue de Tervuren that starts from the Palais du Cinquantenaire (see entry).

Location
15 Steenweg op Leuven
B-1980 Tervuren

Bus
NL from Brussels' North Station

Musée Royal de l'Afrique Centrale in Tervuren

Musée Royal de l'Afrique Centrale

Musée Royal de l'Afrique Centrale•
(1898–1960 'Musée du Congo')

Central Africa Museum
in Tervuren

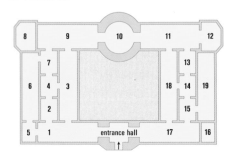

1 Agriculture and mining
2 Wood (Xylothèque)
3 Belgium and Central Africa
4 Europe and Central Africa
5 Jewellery and handicrafts
6 Rest of Africa
7 Central African sculptures
8 (Being reorganised)
9 Central African ethnography
10 Rotunda (statues)
11 Comparative ethnography
12 Zoological dioramas
13 Insects and other invertebrates
14 Fish, amphibians and reptiles
15 Birds
16 (Being reorganised)
17 Mammals
18 Prehistory and archaeology
19 Mineralogy

Tram
44 from Square Montgomery

Distance
18 km (11 miles) SE
(via Avenue de Tervuren)

Opening times
16 Mar.–15 Oct. daily
9 a.m.–5. 30 p.m.
16 Oct.–15 Mar. daily
10 a.m.–4.30 p.m.

Free admission

The museum is housed in a palatial building designed by the French architect Charles Girault. It was commissioned by King Leopold II and opened by King Albert in 1910. It is aimed mainly at those particularly interested in Central Africa but also appeals to anyone whose hobby is anthropology, biology, mineralogy or archaeology.

On average 250,000 people visit the museum every year and because of its lovely setting and fine architecture it has become one of the main attractions in the Brussels area.

All 20 rooms can be visited but the number may vary since constant alterations are in progress. The museum contains an impressive collection of masks and sculptures (including many items from the former Belgian Congo, now Zaire), weapons, tools, objects of wood and ivory, souvenirs of voyages of discovery and of the colonial period, samples of soil and rock, models of dwellings, casts of the native population, busts, stuffed and preserved animals (including birds and insects; fine butterfly collection), dioramas showing particular animals in their natural surroundings, models showing mining operations, etc.

Parc de Tervuren

South of the museum, beyond a pretty terraced garden laid out in the French style with ponds and flower-beds, is the 234 ha (578 acre) Park de Tervuren, one of the most popular areas for the people of Brussels. The park has a superb arboretum, fine lawns and a boating-lake overlooked by the Baroque Chapel of St Hubert built in 1617.

South-west of the park is the ancient village of Tervuren. About 6 km (4 miles) south-west of Tervuren is the little village of Jezus-Eik on the edge of the Forêt de Soignes (see entry), with many eating-places, Kriek-Lambic being their speciality.

Musées Royaux des Beaux-Arts de Belgique   D3
(Belgian Royal Museum of Fine Arts)

After lengthy renovation work on the old museum buildings and the completion of a new subterranean building, the autumn of 1984 saw the opening of an art museum that is one of the greatest of its kind in the world.

The nucleus of the present museum is an art collection which in 1797 was housed in the former palace of Charles of Lorraine. During the Napoleonic period Brussels experienced a genuine upsurge of interest in the arts which eventually led to the founding of the Royal Museum of Fine Arts in 1846.

Location
3 Rue de la Régence

Trams
92, 94

Buses
20, 34, 35, 71, 96

Work on the Palais des Beaux-Arts, designed by Alphonse Balat, began in 1874. It is an elegant building in the Classical style and today houses the Musée d'Art Ancien, the collection of Old Masters and 19th c. works.

Musée d'Art Ancien

The year 1978 saw the start of work on the subterranean new building for the Modern Art collection. The architect Roger Bastin has created a huge underground museum complex which has enabled the former Palais Altenloh to be preserved and restored. An original feature of the new building is a semicircular light well opening on to the attractive Place du Musée.

Musée d'Art Moderne

The old and new museum buildings, together with the Palais Altenloh, provide well over 20,000 sq. m (215,200 sq. ft) of exhibition space.

In 1984 the Royal Collections comprised almost 17,000 works, including 1573 Old Masters, 2660 paintings by 19th and 20th c. artists, well over 7000 prints and more than 1700 pieces of sculpture.

Among the museum's treasures are 15th and 16th c. works including Old Masters by the Master of Flémalle, Bruegel, Rubens and Jordaens. The Italian school of the same period is represented by Crivelli, Tintoretto, Crespi, Tiepolo, etc. Cranach is the most important representative of the German Old Masters and Ribera of the Spanish. Works by the Master of Aix, Jan Hay, Vouet, Champaigne and others form the nucleus of the collection of French Old Masters.

15th–16th c.

The 16th, 17th and 18th c. Dutch school is widely represented, from Bosch to Hals, from Van Heemskerck to Rembrandt and Van Goyen.

17th–18th c.

Neo-Classicism (including Navez), Romanticism (including Wappers and Gallail), Realism (including Stevens Brothers, Artan, Laermans) are represented in the 19th c. Art section, as are David, Delacroix, Courbet and Burne-Jones.

19th c.

The 20th c. Art section covers works by James Ensor, Spillaert and Rik Wouters, Flemish Expressionists such as Permeke, De Smet and Frits Van den Berghe and the Surrealists Magritte, Mesens and Delvaux.

20th c.

There is a general survey of the post-1945 generations of artists – ranging from the new Belgian school to the movements of the present day – with works by Max Ernst, Dalí, Tanguy, Vasarely, etc.

post–1945

71

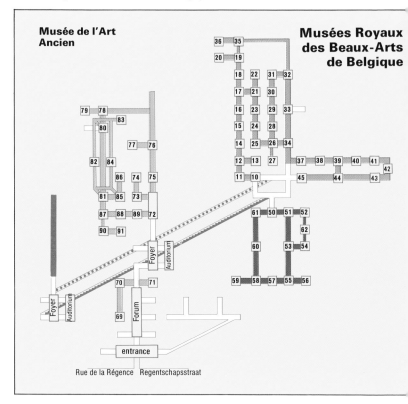

Musée de l'Art Ancien

Musées Royaux des Beaux-Arts de Belgique

Foyer
Auditorium
Foyer
Auditorium
Forum

entrance

Rue de la Régence   Regentschapsstraat

15th and 16th century
10–17, 21–34 Old Dutch school
    10–17 Flemish Primitives
       11 Van der Weyden
       13 Bouts
       14 Memling
       17 Bosch
    21–34 16th c. Flemish school
       22 Metsys
       24 Mostaert
       25 Gossart
       26 Van Orley
       31 Bruegel
       32 Moro
       34 Bril
  17, 24, 25 North Dutch school
    18–20 German school
       20 Cronach
11, 12, 15, 16 French school
    37–45 Delporte Bequest

17th and 18th century
52–54, 57–60 Flemish school
       62 Rubens
       50 Spanish school
       61 French school
       60 Dutch school
    50–51 Italian school (14th–18th c.)

19th century
    69–70 Neo-Classicism Romanticism
    72–80 Realism
       79 Meunier
    82–84 Water-colours, drawings
    80–85 Symbolism
       87 Liminism
       88 Evenepoel
       89 First Laethem school
    90–91 Impressionism
       91 Hess-Vandenbroeck Bequest

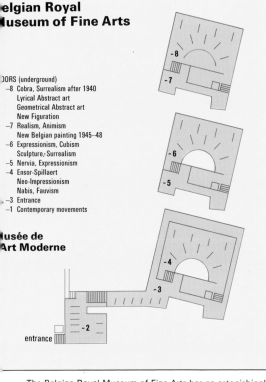

**elgian Royal
useum of Fine Arts**

OORS (underground)
−8 Cobra, Surrealism after 1940
    Lyrical Abstract art
    Geometrical Abstract art
    New Figuration
−7 Realism, Animism
    New Belgian painting 1945–48
−6 Expressionism, Cubism
    Sculpture, Surrealism
−5 Nervia, Expressionism
−4 Ensor-Spillaert
    Neo-Impressionism
    Nabis, Fauvism
−3 Entrance
−1 Contemporary movements

**usée de
Art Moderne**

−4
−3
−2
entrance

The Belgian Royal Museum of Fine Arts has an astonishingly   Sculptures
rich sculpture collection ranging from the 17th to the 20th c.
The 19th c. is particularly well represented with works by
Godecharle, Geefs, Meunier, Rodin, De Vigne, Minne, etc.

Fine arts on display

There are important 20th c. works by Bourdelle, Maillol,
Wouters, Arp, Marini, Jespers, Moore, Zadkine, Richier,
Laurens and Schöffer.

The large collection of drawings covers works ranging from   Drawings
Bruegel the Elder, Rembrandt, Jordaens and Van Gogh to Van
Ostade, Spranger and Dotremont.

Apart from the Museum's own treasures it has several   Bequests
important bequests including those of De Grez (1914; 4249
works), Della Faille de Leverghem (1942; 37 paintings) and

Fine arts on display

Pieter Bruegel's "Fall of Icarus" in the Musée d'Art Ancien

Exhibition hall

Delporte-Livrauw (1973; 225 works). A whole series of other patrons and artists have also helped to make this currently one of the finest art museums in the world.

Notre-Dame au Finistère

See Rue Neuve

Notre-Dame au Sablon

See Notre-Dame du Sablon

*Notre-Dame aux Riches Claires (church)   C3

The Church of Notre-Dame aux Riches Claires is an architectural masterpiece. Built in the 17th c. Flemish-Italian style, and then considerably enlarged in the 19th c., it was originally the work of the master builder Luc Faid'Herbe.
Of especial note is the magnificent Altar of Notre-Dame des Sept Douleurs (Our Lady of the Seven Sorrows), with its embroidery and Brussels lace and a much loved Pietà probably dating from the 16th c.
There is a big annual pilgrimage to the church on the third Sunday in September.

Location
Rue des Riches Claires

Metro station
Bourse

*Notre-Dame de la Chapelle (church)   D3

The Church of Notre-Dame de la Chapelle (Our lady of the Chapel) is right next to the old working-class district of Brussels known as Les Marolles (see entry). From its very beginning it has been surrounded by bustling merchants and craftsmen, and throughout the centuries it has remained one of the most popular places of worship in Brussels.
Building work on the church was begun about 1190 on the site of a Romanesque baptistery founded in 1134 by Godefroy I, Duke of Brabant. The choir and transept are in the Romanesque-Gothic transitional style and the nave is pure Gothic, having been built between 1421 and 1483. The west tower, crowned by a Baroque cupola, was not completed until 1699.
The history of the building of the church has much in common with that of the Cathedral of St Michael (see St Michel) and both have the same typically Brabant-Gothic internal and external features.
The different building and architectural styles mingle harmoniously in this church and make it one of Belgium's most interesting religious buildings.

In order to get a good idea of this building and its special features it is advisable to walk round the outside of the church before going inside. In this way the visitor will discover the

Location
Place de la Chapelle

Buses
20, 21, 34, 38, 71, 95, 96

Trams
92, 93, 94

Opening times
15 June–15 Oct.: daily
10.30 a.m.–12.30 p.m. and
2–5 p.m.; rest of year during
services only

Exterior

oldest part of the church – the Chapelle Ste-Croix between the choir and the transept on the south side, with its little round Romanesque tower. The grimacing heads on the frieze of the south portal and over the buttresses of the choir and the gargoyles around the church make quite an amusing study.

Interior

The most impressive feature to meet the eye in the mystical-seeming interior of the church is the nave, consecrated in 1434, with its huge columns and delicate Late Gothic triforium.
As in St Michel (see entry), the figures of the Apostles (17th c.) are largely by J. Duquesnoy the Elder and L. Faid'Herbe. The carved wooden pulpit (early 18th c.) is by P.-D. Plumier.
The windows and wall-paintings in the Romanesque-Gothic choir (12th–13th c.) date from the 16th c.
On a pillar to the left of the choir is a monument to Duke Charles Alexandre de Croy (d. 1624) who was murdered by his page-boy; on the other side is a tablet commemorating Frans Anneessens, who is buried here.
In the chapel behind the choir can be found the marble Tomb of the Spinola family (18th c) and five 17th c. landscape-paintings.

Aisles

In the chapels of the Late Gothic aisles (15th c.) are numerous works of art, including some splendid religious paintings (17th c.) and the fine wood-carving of St Anne with the Madonna and Child (17th c.).
The great painter Pieter Bruegel the Elder (d. 1596 – see Famous People) is buried in the Chapel of Notre-Dame du Rosaire (fourth on the right of the main portal); opposite the chapel altar is a memorial erected by his son Jan "the Velvet" and above it is a copy of the original picture painted for the church by Rubens as a tribute to Bruegel but sold in Amsterdam in 1765 (frame and inscription by Bruegel's grandson David Teniers III).
In the second chapel to the left of the main portal is the much-venerated Our Lady of the Solitude, her head draped with a black lace mantilla; the figure was brought here in the early 17th c. by the Infanta Isabella.

Area around Notre-Dame de la Chapelle

Maison Bruegel

A market is held every morning in the Place de la Chapelle in front of the church. Leading off from this square is the Rue Haute where, at No. 132 (Maison Bruegel), currently closed, Pieter Bruegel spent the last years of his life (see Famous People).

Former Brigittine church
(Eglise des Brigittines)

Also only a few yards from the church is the former Brigittine church (1663–72; restored 1864–74). Its splendid façade in the Flemish-Italian style with its harmonious proportions and fine decoration is particularly beautiful when illuminated in the evening. This former place of worship is now a cultural centre.

Tour d'Angle (Tour
Anneessens)

It is also worth making a small detour to the Tour Anneessens, a relic of Brussels' first city wall (late 13th c.; once 4 km (2·5 miles) long, with seven gates and some 50 defensive towers).

Notre-Dame de la Chapelle, one of Brussels' most popular churches ▶

Frans Anneessens, the Elder of the Guild of Brussels Craftsmen, is said to have been held prisoner in this tower in 1719. Anneessens was beheaded in the Grand'Place (see entry) for having defended the privileges of the guilds.

Notre-Dame de Laeken (church)   B3

Location
Parvis Notre-Dame de Laeken (top of Avenue de la Reine)

Metro station
Bockstael

Bus
53

Trams
81, 94

The huge Church of Notre-Dame de Laeken (Our Lady of Laeken) was planned by King Leopold I in 1851, on the death of his wife Louise-Marie of Orléans, as a burial-place for the Belgian royal family. The international competition to design it was won by Joseph Poelaert, a young architect who was later to become famous (see Palais de Justice). The foundation-stone was laid in 1854 and the church was consecrated in 1872. The German architect von Schmidt was responsible for the façade, the portals and the completion of the main tower (early 19th c.).
The church is in the Early Gothic style but has the generous proportions of High Gothic. On the High Altar is a much-venerated statue of the Madonna (Notre-Dame de Laeken, 13th c.); behind the choir is the royal crypt (open to visitors from April to the end of October on Sundays between 3 and 5 p.m.).

Cemetery

In the interesting cemetery, with its graves of prominent Belgians, still stands the choir of the old Church of Laeken (13th c), an interesting example of pure Early Gothic style.

Notre-Dame du Bon Secours (church)   C3

Location
Rue du Marché au Charbon

Metro station
Ste-Catherine

The Church of Notre-Dame du Bon Secours in the Rue du Marché au Charbon (coal market) is one of the finest examples of Flemish Renaissance architecture. It was built between 1664 and 1694 on the site of a former poorhouse church. The main tower is unusual, having a hexagonal ground-plan and short side aisles. On the High Altar, made in 1705 to a design by J.-P. Van Baurscheit, is a much-venerated 16th c. statue of the Madonna.

Notre-Dame du Finistère

See Rue Neuve

*Notre-Dame du Sablon (church)   D3

Location
Rue de la Régence (between Place du Petit Sablon and Place du Grand Sablon)

Buses
20, 34, 48, 95, 96

Notre-Dame du Sablon or, to give it its correct name, Notre-Dame des Victoires (Our Lady of Victories), one of Belgium's most beautiful Late Gothic churches, stands, in perfect harmony with its setting, between the peace and quiet of the two squares, Le Petit and Le Grand Sablon.
It was built in the 15th c. (choir 1436, nave completed in the 16th c.; restored in the late 19th c.) on the site of the Guild

of the Crossbowmen's Chapel (see Practical Information – Crossbowmen) which had stood in this sandy wasteland (sablon) since 1304.

Trams
92, 94

The miraculous healing statuette of Our Lady was brought here by boat to the Chapel of the Crossbowmen in 1348 after it had been stolen from Antwerp Cathedral by a pious woman, Baert Soetens, at the behest of the Virgin Mary who had appeared to her in a vision. It was later to be borne in grand procession round the church by the Duke and his eldest son, thus giving rise to the tradition of the Ommegang (procession) still repeated in the Grand'Place (see entry) in July every year (see Practical Information – Calendar of Events).

The church has magnificent stained-glass windows, illuminated at night, and its nave and four aisles are filled with works of art, including the Gothic carvings on the corner-stones, the wall-paintings in the choir dating from 1435 and the Late Gothic tabernacle and Adoration of the Magi in the sacrarium (1549).

Interior

The miraculous statue of Our Lady stands in front of the left choir column, and there are three versions of its journey by boat in the church: in the 15th c. keystone (left transept), in a sculpture (right transept) and on the stucco canopy of the organ.

There is a handsome Baroque pulpit, carved by Marcus de Vos (1697), supported by the Evangelical symbols of Matthew, Mark, Luke and John. There are other fine 17th c. marble monuments and paintings and a statue of St Ursula.

The Baroque side chapels were endowed by the Tour et Tassis family (see Musée Instrumental), founders of the postal service.

Place du Petit Sablon and Notre-Dame du Sablon

Palais des Académies

<table>
<tr><td>Place du Grand Sablon</td><td>The Sablon (sand) was originally a sandy wasteland and was used in the 13th c. as a burial-ground for the St-Jean Hospice until the building of the Crossbowmen's Chapel here in 1304. In the 16th c. noble families such as d'Egmont, Culembourg, Bréderode and Tour et Tassis started making the Sablon their home and it became an elegant residential area.
At the week-end, from 10 a.m. until 6 p.m. on Saturdays and until 4 p.m. on Sundays, the Grand Sablon is the venue for the popular open-air antiques market (Marché des Antiquités et des Livres) in front of the church.</td></tr>
<tr><td>Place du Petit Sablon</td><td>The pretty little Place du Petit Sablon is an enclosed 19th c. square, made particularly attractive by the wrought iron that surrounds it, with each of the 48 small columns supporting charming little bronze statues representing the 16th c. guilds. The upper exit from the Petit Sablon leads to the Palais Egmont (see entry).</td></tr>
</table>

Palais des Académies (Academy Palace)   D4

Location
Place des Palais

Buses
20, 34, 38, 48, 71, 95, 96

Trams
92, 93, 94

Between the Parc de Bruxelles and the Palais Royal is the Palais des Académies, home of the Académie Royale des Sciences, des Lettres et des Beaux-Arts (Academy of Science, Literature and Fine Arts) and the Académie de Médecine with their libraries of precious books.

When the mansion of the Prince of Orange (Rue de la Loi) was burnt down in 1820 the nation decided to offer the young, very popular Prince a magnificent residence. The architect van der Straeten designed it, Suys built it, and the Prince provided the luxurious furnishings: parquet floors of rare woods, costly marble, lapis lazuli tables and the finest silk wall-coverings brought the total cost of the furnishings to no less that an estimated 20 million francs. The Prince returned to Holland after the 1830 Revolution and everything he left behind was confiscated until 1842 when his property was restored to him. The palace, however, he made over to the Belgian State.

The palace was restored in 1860 and came to house the Museum of Modern Art. In 1872 it became the seat of the Academy, which had been founded by the Empress Maria-Theresa. It is here that the Royal Academy of French Language and Literature ceremonially receives new members, as when Colette formally welcomed Anne de Noailles and Cocteau did the same for Colette. Queen Elisabeth of Belgium, instigator of the great musical competition, has always honoured this gathering with her presence.

The Academy Palace is surrounded by a large elegant garden full of statues and other works of art.

*Palais des Beaux-Arts (Palace of Fine Arts)   D3/4

Location
10 Rue Royale and 23 Rue Ravenstein

Metro stations
Parc, Gare Centrale

The extensive building complex of the Palais des Beaux-Arts, in the centre of Brussels between Rue Royale and Rue Ravenstein, is the most important cultural centre in Brussels. It has exhibition rooms, theatres, concert-halls and conference rooms, is the seat of several cultural institutes such as the Musée du Cinéma, and much else besides.

The complex was built between 1922 and 1929, having been designed by Victor Horta, Belgium's leading Art Nouveau architect, and covers an area of 1 ha (2½ acres) between the Lower and the Upper Town. The architect skilfully exploited the sloping nature of the land by building on different levels.

There are three principal storeys. The top storey (entrance Rue Royale) is taken up by exhibition rooms (with cafeteria), the middle one (entrance Rue Ravenstein) contains the reception concourse and the Centre d'Animation for cultural activities, while serving as the entrance to the facilities for concerts, theatres and conferences on the ground floor (Henry Le Bœuf Hall for 2200 spectators, with highly praised acoustics and large organ).

Besides temporary art exhibitions (information on subjects and dates in the daily papers) this is also the venue for concerts by the Belgian National Orchestra and performances by the Théâtre du Rideau (Tuesday matinées at 12.40 p.m. in winter, known as Midis de Théâtre).

There is a particularly large number of cultural events at weekends, especially in the evening – lectures and concerts, theatre and film performances, dance, singing, amateur groups and avant-garde works.

The Palais des Beaux-Arts is of interest both to an artist wanting to mount his own exhibition and to those seeking culture in an active or a passive capacity.

The palace also houses the Musée du Cinéma (Cinema Museum; entrance 9 Rue du Baron Horta). There is an interesting exhibition on the development of the art of the cinema, and several daily showings of old movies (the silent ones with piano accompaniment!). The current programme can be found out by telephoning 5134155.

Musée du Cinéma

The complex also houses the offices of various cultural institutes such as the Concours Musical Reine Elisabeth, the Société Philharmonique de Bruxelles, Europalia, AdAC (Association des Arts et de la Culture), etc.

Institutes

Buses
20, 21, 34, 38, 71, 95, 96

Trams
92, 93, 94

Opening times
Mon.–Sat. 10 a.m.–10 p.m.;
Sun. 10 a.m.–6 p.m.

Palais Berlaymont (European Communities Building)

D5

At the east end of the Rue de la Loi leading from the city centre to the Palais du Cinquantenaire (see entry) stand the Berlaymont, as it is known, the huge Common Market building that houses the Commission, the administrative arm of the European Communities. The Palais Berlaymont, with its irregular cruciform ground plan, has a certain elegance despite its size. It was built between 1963 and 1969 and designed by de Vestel.

Brussels has been the seat of the European Communities since 1958. Before the Berlaymont was built the various Brussels-based Community organs (EEC Commission, Euratom) had their offices in different buildings throughout the city. The organs of what was then the Community of the Six were brought together in 1967 and combined as far as possible in the Berlaymont.

The growing membership f the EEC has meant that today the

Location
Rond-Point Robert Schuman

Metro station
Schuman

Guided tours
by arrangment
(tel. 235 11 11)

Berlaymont – the EEC building in Robert Schuman Square

new building is also threatening to burst at the seams and the Charlemagne tower block has had to be built next door to it to house some of the 8000 (!) Eurocrats.

*Palais du Cinquantenaire   D5
(with the Royal Museums of Art and History and the Army Museum)

Location
Parc du Cinquantenaire
(Etterbeek)

Metro station
Merode

Buses
20, 28, 36, 80

Trams
62, 81

The Palais du Cinquantenaire (Palace of the Fiftieth Anniversary) houses one of the biggest museums of military history anywhere in the world, both in terms of the number of rooms and the volume and variety of the collections. The Palais du Cinquantenaire also houses the antiquities collection of the Royal Museums of Art and History, a transport museum and the Collection of Arts and Crafts.

The focal point of the complex is its triumphal arch, designed by the architect Charles Girault in 1904–5, which has three arches of equal height surmounted by a Roman chariot drawn by four bronze horses. Female figures at the base of the arches represent Belgium's provinces. The palace is enclosed by two colonnades.

Along the back walls of the colonnades there are 36 mosaic tablets extolling the glories of Belgium. The left wing houses the Royal Army Museum and the right wing contains the Royal Museum of Art and History.

Park

The palace is surrounded by a 37·5 ha (93 acre) park, laid out for the national exhibition held to celebrate 50 years of independence.

The triumphal arch, focal point of the Palais du Cinquantenaire

The park contains monuments and statues, including Constantin Meunier's "Reaper" and the famous relief by Jef Lambeaux, "Human Passions", kept in one of the first pavilions built by Horta.

The Moorish building with a minaret was built for the national exhibition in 1880. The panorama of Cairo was painted by E. Wauters. This splendid building, altered and modernised, has, since 1978, been the Islamic Cultural Centre and has a mosque alongside it.

The art conservation and restoration institute lies to the left of the park.

*Musée Royal de l'Armée et d'Histoire Militaire
(Royal Museum of the Army and Military History)

The Royal Museum of the Army and Military History provides a general impression of the major military and historical events that have taken place on Belgian soil since the Brabant Revolution of 1789. There are various uniforms, orders and decorations, standards and an extensive collection of weapons. The adjoining military archives and their picture room give the visitor a vivid impression of the history of the defence of Belgium.

Opening times
9–midday, 1–4.45 p.m. (summer); 9–midday, 1–4 p.m. (winter)

Closed
Mon, and most public holidays

The Aviation section is in a huge room containing an extraordinary collection of First World War fighter planes, the unforgettable Spitfires that took part in the Battle of Britain (1940) and a special collection of models of powered aircraft

Aviation section

83

Part of the Palais du Cinquantenaire: Musée Royal de l'Armée et d'Histoire Militaire

from 1912 to the present day. The visitor can also see gondolas from balloons and airships.

Armoured car section

The armoured car section of this military museum is one of the most interesting collections of its kind in Europe. The most impressive exhibits are a Mk IV Churchill tank, a T13 and a Flak 8.8. There are also many other tanks and pieces of artillery on display, most of which were used in the First or Second World War.

*Musées Royaux d'Art et d'Histoire
(Royal Museums of Art and History)

Opening times
9.30 a.m.–12.30 p.m. and
1.30–5 p.m. Sat. and Sun.
10 a.m.–5 p.m.

The Royal Museums of Art and History house collections of antiquities, arts and crafts, ethnological objects, national folklore and items from prehistory and the Belgium of the past.
Closed Mon. and most public holidays.
The collections are currently being rearranged, which means that many of the rooms are temporarily closed or have changed opening times. The sections currently open on even dates are: Middle East, Egypt, Greece, Rome; on uneven dates: arts and crafts, tapestries, lace, glass paintings, precision instruments, ceramics, jewellery and toys.

Kennedy Wing

The Kennedy Wing contains pre-Christian antiquities from the Middle East, arranged according to country and period: Palestine, Cyprus, Mesopotamia, Persia, Syria, Phoenicia and pre-Islamic Arabia.

Palais du Cinquantenaire

Musées Royaux d'Art et d'Histoire

Royal Museums of Art and History

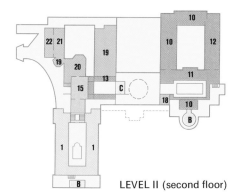

LEVEL II (second floor)

LEVEL I (first floor)

Avenue de la Chevalerie

Avenue des Nerviens

Avenue J.F. Kennedy

Parc du Cinquantenaire

LEVEL 0 (ground floor)

Level	Room	
		THE ANCIENT WORLD
II	1	Egypt
0	2	Near and Middle East
I	3	Greece
I	4	Roman Empire
0	5	Model of the city of Rome
I	6	Colonnade and mosaics from Apamea
0	7	BELGIAN ARCHAEOLOGY
		EUROPEAN ARTS AND CRAFTS
I	8	Sculpture, furniture, tapestries
I	8a	Art from the Meuse area
I	9	Silver, metal objects Measuring instruments
I+II	10	Ceramics
II	11	Lace
II	12	Textiles
I+II	13	Glass
I	14	FOLKLORE
II	15	EUROPEAN HANDICRAFTS
0	16	TRANSPORT MUSEUM
		NON-EUROPEAN CIVILIZATIONS
I	17	Islam
I+II	18	Christian art from the East
I+II	19	South-east Asia
I+II	20	Far East
I+II	21	Pre-Columbian America
I+II	22	Oceania
I	23	MUSEUM FOR THE BLIND
		GENERAL SERVICES
0	A	Workshops
I+II	B	Libraries
I+II	C	Lecture rooms
I	D	Slide library
0+I	E	Temporary exhibitions
I	F	Schools service

85

This section is adjoined by the Georges Dossin Assyriological Foundation (Fondation Assyriologique) which aims at promoting scientific research in the fields of Middle-Eastern history, epigraphy, language and archaeology.

Ground floor:
On the ground floor is a model of Rome as it was in the 4th c. AD.

First floor:
On the first floor are the Greek, Etruscan and Roman collections. The reconstruction of the colonnade which lined the main street of the Syrian town of Apamea in the 2nd c. AD requires a large room all to itself. The mosaics below the colonnade date back to AD 469. The hall is dominated by a bronze statue of Septimius Severus. Belgian excavations between 1930 and 1938 made it possible to bring back an important mosaic with magnificent hunting scenes. The Greek exhibits in the geometrical rooms are also presented in chronological order. Exhibits in the Roman gallery include marble sarcophagi, Phrygian stelae, statues, glass, terracota lamps and a special Etruscan collection. A whole room is devoted to portraying daily life in Greece and Rome. The Belgian archaeological research cente, working in Apamea to uncover further traces of the town, also comes under this department.
The Egyptian antiquities take up 13 rooms and cover all periods of Egyptian civilisation. The East Wing contains several important monuments from various periods.
Adjoining this section are the Queen Elisabeth Egyptological Foundation (Fondation Egyptologique Reine Elisabeth) and an extensive library.

Nervia Wing

Islam:
This large collection of ceramics illustrates this important branch of Islamic art, principally by means of exhibits from Persia, Mesopotamia and Anatolia. It also contains weapons, glass, musical instruments, miniatures and a few Persian reptiles.

Eastern Greek art:
One room is devoted to Eastern Greek art, with Byzantine exhibits, icons and Russian and East European religious objects.

Far East:
Newly renovated rooms contain Far Eastern art, arranged in temporary exhibitions on specific themes so as to illustrate a particular aspect of the period in question.
One room is devoted to Cambodia and contains a whole series of exquisite Khmer sculptures dating from the 10th–12th c.
Another room contains items from excavations in China and Korea. Two rooms are devoted to the Japanese collections of painting, porcelain, weapons, masks, Noh theatre costumes and lacquerwork. The room containing pictures and world-famous books may be visited only by prior arrangement.
Adjoining this section is the Institut Belge des Hautes Etudes Chinoises (Belgian Institute of Sinology), and important Sino-Buddhist centre and the only one in Brussels.

The Musées Royaux d'Art et d'Histoire in the Palais du Cinquantenaire

America:
America is the theme of seven Pre-Columbian and ethnological rooms, displaying treasures from the Aztecs, from Central America, the Mayas, Mexico and Peru. Also on display is a remarkable cloak of red feathers worked by the Tupinamba Indians of Brazil.

India, South-east Asia:
Seven rooms are devoted to India and South-east Asia. Besides numerous *objets d'art* there is also a collection of contemporary glass.

Belgian folk art:
Belgian folk art takes up seven rooms. Among the exhibits are reconstuctions of an old Brussels chemist's shop and of a meeting room of the Guild of St Sebastian, collections of traditional religious art and magic, memorabilia of former guilds, hand tools used for making traditional textiles, old cooking moulds, models of windmills, etc.

Silver:
The collection of the work of Belgian silversmiths shows the development in style from the 17th to the 19th c.
Some very fine 16th and 17th c. pieces are examples of silverware made for the Church and of the demand for sumptuous silver for more mundane purposes, for drinking-vessels in particular.
In the 18th and early 19th c. the range of silver tableware was enlarged by the introduction of special hot chocolate, coffee and tea services so that these newly introduced drinks could be sipped in style.

Palais d'Egmont

One room is reserved for the non-precious metals that were mainly used in the making of censers, crosses, statues, bronze items, etc. There is also a range of exquisite articles in pewter.

Handicrafts:
Several rooms have exhibitions of modern art from several West European countries. These include art deco pieces and a stone carved and painted by Paul Gauguin.

Scientific instruments:
One whole room is devoted exclusively to 16th and 17th c. scientific instruments.

Porcelain:
The porcelain is on display in a rotunda and includes the remarkable collection of porcelain from Tournai.

Further collections:
Other rooms contain collections of sculpture, carpets, lace, medieval costumes and mosaic items.
Five rooms are devoted to depicting the development of "ancient Belgium" and to objects dating from the Belgo-Roman period.
There is also an impressive collection of ceramic and hand-crafted sculptures, housed in about 20 rooms.

Palais d'Egmont (Egmont Palace) D3

Location
Rue aux Laines

Buses
20, 34, 48, 71, 95, 96

Trams
92, 94

The Palais d'Egmont, or Arenberg Palace, stands at one end of the Place du Petit Sablon (see Notre-Dame du Sablon). It was acquired by the city of Brussels in 1918 and today houses departments of the Ministry of Foreign Affairs.
The Princess of Gavre, widow of Count Jean d'Egmont, bought the first piece of land here in 1532 and built a mansion (Hôtel) that became known as the Little Egmont Palace. By buying up neighbouring sites she was able to enlarge the property into the Grand Hôtel d'Egmont. After Count Lamoral Egmont was tried and beheaded the building was seized by the Spanish King.
Over the centuries the palace has experienced fires, rebuilding and internal alterations. After the Arenberg-Egmont family had relinquished their ownership the city of Brussels acquired it in 1918. In 1964 the Belgian State became its new owner and it was handed over to the Ministry of Foreign Affairs.

Exterior

The Antwerp architect H. van Kuyck was entrusted with the restoration and alterations. As it appears at present, the walls, pavilion and portal are by Sevandoni (1760–62), as is the gallery. The wings have been altered several times since the 16th c.: the left wing, the riding-school, the stables and the rear of the building facing the garden are by T. Suys; the right wing and the right-hand corner of the main part of the building are by Flammeau and Girault. – The façade is decorated with rectangular pilasters and Ionic columns. The magnificent marble steps of the right wing are a copy of the steps of the Embassy at Versailles. The two marble sculptures at the foot of these steps are "The Rape of Proserpine" and "The Rape of the Sabines".

View of the Palais d'Egmont

The reconstructed salons have been either furnished in the   Interior
sumptuous 18th c. style or entirely modernised, depending on
their new function. The grand hall in the ring wing has a painted
ceiling and four Brussels tapestries (Four Continents) on its
upper panels. This is where Claude Volter, the actor and
director, very successfully staged his first plays. The famous
people that have stayed in the palace have included Queen
Christine of Sweden, Louis XV, the French poet Jean-Baptiste
Rousseau and Voltaire.

The other rooms are decorated with exquisite wall-hangings
and wooden panelling. The wainscotting from the former
library is now in the Press Conference Room.

The hall of mirrors on the first floor has 35 m (115 ft) of wall
panelling in rare woods. The old riding-school has been turned
into offices and a hall for international conferences.

Part of the garden behind the building is open to the public.   Garden
Among its statues is a replica of the figure of Peter Pan in
London's Kensington Gardens.

The garden has access to the Rue aux Laines, Rue du Grand
Cerf and the Boulevard de Waterloo.

*Palais de Justice (Law Courts)   D3

The Palais de Justice (Law Courts) dominates the Brussels   **Location**
skyline. It was the biggest building erected in the 19th c.   Place Poelaert
(1866–83) and was designed by Joseph Poelaert (d. 1879).   **Trams**
It cost over 50 million Belgian francs and covers an area of   92, 94

Palais de la Nation

The Palais de Justice from the Palais Royal

26,000 sq. m (280,000 sq. ft (St Peter's in Rome 15,160 sq. m (163,000 sq. ft)).

Above the massive building the central dome soars to a height of 104 m (341 ft) above the level of the square. The rooms inside house Belgium's supreme lawcourts and it has a vast foyer.

The Palais de Justice stands on the site of the medieval gallows where common criminals were executed until well into the 16th c.

*Palais de la Nation   C4

Location
16 Rue de la Loi

Metro station
Parc

Trams
92, 93, 94

The Palais de la Nation was built for the Supreme Council in the Classical style in the late 18th c. and was designed by the famous French architect Barnabé Guimard. It is now the Belgian Parliament building and houses the Senate and Chamber of Deputies.

Its façade overlooking the attractive Parc de Bruxelles has a Classical gable by Gilles-Lambert Godecharle.

*Palais Royal (also: Palais du Roi; King's Palace)   D4

Location
Place des Palais

Metro station
Luxembourg, Parc

The most important building in the Quartier Royal is the King's Palace. Although the King does not live there (see Château Royal de Laeken) it is his official town residence for ceremonies and receptions.

The palace stands on the site of the old ducal castle which burnt

View of the Palais Royal

down in 1731. It is made up of two 18th c. pavilion-type residences, once separated by a street. These were linked by a central building in 1827–29 after William I, the Dutch King, became Regent of the United Netherlands and took up residence in Brussels. The palace was given its final form by King Leopold II, who started to enlarge it in 1904 and commissioned the architect Henri Maquet to design a Louis XVI façade (the gable over the central colonnade has an allegory of Belgium by the sculptor Th. Vinçotte).

The rooms inside are very fine and their rich furnishings include magnificent Bohemian crystal chandeliers and valuable paintings.

The changing of the guard takes place every day at 2.30 p.m. to the sound of drums.

Opposite the King's Palace is the Parc de Bruxelles, a formal park open to the public which was once a hunting preserve belonging to the Dukes of Brabant. It has fountains, charming statues, and, in the summer, open-air concerts.

North of the park, in Rue de la Loi, is the Palais de la Nation (see entry), the Belgian Parliament building.

The Théâtre Royal du Parc (Royal Park Theatre) in the north-east corner of the park dates from 1782 and is one of the capital's classical theatres.

The Musée de la Dynastie (Dynasty Museum; open Wed. and Sat. 2–5 p.m.) is at 21 Rue Bréderode, behind the Palais Royal.

The Place Royale, west of the Palais Royal, on the Coudenberg (Cold Mount), was once the seat of the sovereigns, and just

Buses
20, 34, 38, 95, 96

Trams
92, 93, 94

Opening times
Tues.–Sat. 10 a.m.–5 p.m. in summer only

Parc de Bruxelles

Théâtre Royal du Parc

Musée de la Dynastie

Place Royale

91

above the terraces of the Mont des Arts. Like the Rue Royale and the other streets around the park, the Place Royale owes its pesent appearance to the Classical-style buildings surrounding it, dating 1173–80, and to their French architect, Barnabé Guinard.

In the middle of the square, with its magnificent views over downtown Brussels, is the impressive equestrian statue put there in 1848 of Godefroy de Bouillon, Duke of Lower Lorraine and Commander of the First Crusade in 1097.

The church with the copper dome on the south-east side of the Place Royale is the Court Church of St-Jacques-sur-Coudenberg (1776–85).

Parc de Bruxelles

See Palais Royal

Parc Léopold

See Quartier Léopold

Place de Brouckère

See Boulevards

Place Rogier   C3/4

Location
N edge of the city centre

Metro station
Rogier

Trams
2, 18, 19, 32, 52, 55, 58, 62,
81, 90, 101, 103

The Place Rogier, which in recent years has become one of the busiest places in the Belgian capital, is the old site of the Porte de Cologne (Cologne Gate) in the walls of the medieval city. It is the point at which several main inner-city roads cross the ring of Outer Boulevards (see entry) and is situated at the end of the Rue Neuve (see entry), the city's main downtown shopping street. It is also an important junction for the suburban lines of the Metro and Premetro.

Centre Rogier

The square is dominated on its north side by the Centre Rogier, known as the Martini Tower because of its huge neon sign, and by the Manhattan Centre on its west side. Both are ultra-modern American-type complexes, over 100 m (328 ft) high, with shops, theatres, cinemas, luxury hotels and several hundred flats and offices.

Entertainment quarter

Behind the Place Rogier, around the Rue du Progrès and the Rue d'Aerschoot at the back of the Gare du Nord, lies Brussels' bright-lights district full of all-night bars, sleazy pubs and similar establishments (watch out for clip joints!).

See Boulevards

See World Trade Centre

The Théâtre Royal du Parc, in the Parc de Bruxelles ▶

Place Royale

See Palais Royale

*Porte de Hal (Hal Gate)   D3

Location
Most southerly point of the
Boulevards Extérieurs

Buses 20, 48

Trams 2, 19, 55, 101, 103

The Porte de Hal (Hal Gate) stands at the south end of the Rue Haute, one of the two main streets in the quarter of Les Marolles (see entry). It is the only part of the 14th c. city wall still standing and part of it was given a new façade by Beyaert in the late 19th c. Part of the original fortified ramparts that still existed were covered over when the Boulevards were laid out.

Musée de la Porte de Hal

Inside the fortified gatehouse is the Musée de la Porte de Hal. The collections of arms and armour in this museum are among the best of their kind in Europe. The old medieval suits of armour and more modern firearms are particularly worth seeing. As the Porte de Hal was once part of the armoury built here by the Duke of Burgundy in 1406 and since many of the museum pieces have remained *in situ* for centuries, the people of Brussels like to maintain that their museum is the oldest one in the world.

Quartier Léopold

Location
SE of Brussels

Tram
93

South of the Rue de la Loi is the elegant Quartier Léopold with its regular street pattern. Its major buildings are grouped around the Place Frère-Orban – the Church of St Joseph (19th c.) to the south and the Palais d'Assche (1880) to the east. In the south part of the Quartier Léopold the Square de Meeus, half of which is actually in Ixelles, is crossed by the Rue du Luxembourgh which comes out in the square in front of the Gare du Quartier Léopold (station). North of the station is the Palais d'Europe.

Parc Léopold

To the east, on the far side of the railway line, is the lovely Parc Léopold which dates from 1852. The upper end of the park is bordered by the Institut Royal des Sciences Naturelles.

Institut Royal des Sciences Naturelles
(Royal Institute of Natural Sciences)

Location
31 Rue Vautier (Ixelles)

Buses
20, 36, 80

Tram
93

Opening times
Winter: 9.30 a.m.–12.30 p.m.
and 2–4 p.m.
Summer: 9.30 a.m.–
12.30 p.m. and 2–5 p.m.

Belgium's Royal Institute of Natural Sciences in the Parc Léopold is one of the capital's most fascinating museums.
It holds an extremely interesting zoologial collection with, in its palaeontology department, 10 skeletons averaging 4·5 m (14·8 ft) in height and 8·5 m (27·9 ft) in length of iguanodons, the giant lizard that moved along like a kangaroo, using its hind legs and tail. The fossils were found in 1877–80 in the chalk-layers in the Belgian coalfield at Bernissart.
Also on view are the skeletons of whales and the prehistoric ichthyosaurus, as well as zoological, mineralogical and anthropological collections.
Some of the rooms are temporarily closed for alterations.

Porte de Hal, all that remains of the city wall ▶

Musée Wiertz

The Musée Wiertz, not far from the Institut Royal des Sciences Naturelles, is the old country seat of the painter Antoine-Joseph Wiertz (1806–65), with an exhibition of his works.

*Rue Neuve   C3

Location
Lower Town

Metro stations
Monnaie, Rogier

The Rue Neuve, nowadays the main shopping street in downtown Brussels, runs from the Place de la Monnaie (see Théâtre de la Monnaie) to the Place Rogier (see entry) and takes up a site that in the Middle Ages was occupied by just a couple of wash-houses and a mass of vegetable gardens. The Rue Neuve itself did not come into existence until the 17th c., with the expansion of the city.

Today the Rue Neuve is a busy pedestrian precinct, lined with department stores, exclusive boutiques and ultra-modern shopping arcades (Galerie du Commerce, Galerie du Nord, Inno, City 2).

About half-way along the Rue Neuve stands the Church of Notre Dame du Finistère built in the Flemish Baroque style in the 18th c. and lovingly restored in the 1960s. It has some valuable works of art.

Saint-Denis à Forest (church)

Location
Square Omer Denis (Forest)

Tram
90

The modest little Church of St-Denis in the Forest district of Brussels is of particular historic and art-historical interest.

In the 7th c. this was the site of a chapel dedicated to St Denis. It was here that St Alène, the daughter of the heathen Lord of Dilbeek, was secretly baptised, whereupon her enraged father had her beaten to death. The miracles that followed her entombment in the chapel finally moved even her father to become a Christian.

The present church was begun about 1250 and its style spans all the periods of Gothic architecture, from Late Romanesque to Renaissance.

The beautiful interior has many valuable works of art including the Tomb of St Alène (probably 11th c.), a carved Christ's triumphal arch (13th c.), valuable reliquaries (15th–16th c.), a four-panelled altar-piece by the Brussels painter van Coninxloo (16th c.) and elaborate wrought-iron screen (17th c.).

Benedictine Abbey

The remains of the former Benedictine Abbey of Forest, founded in 1106, which lie behind the church (entrance Place St-Denis) are also worth a visit. The abbey was burned down in 1764, was partially rebuilt and then subsequently dissolved in 1789. Since 1965. it has served the parish of Forest as a cultural centre.

Saint-Jean-Baptiste au Béguinage (Beguine Church)   C3

Location
Place du Béguinage

Metro station
Ste-Catherine

This church, designed by L. Faid'Herbe and built between 1657 and 1676, is one of Belgium's finest Flemish-Italian Baroque buildings and is all that is left of a Beguine convent founded in the 13th c.

It is in a densely populated district of the western Old Town and even from a distance attracts the eye with its splendid triple-gabled façade (restored in 1856; illuminated in the evening).

Its ground-plan and structure are Gothic and its ornamentation and furnishings Baroque. Even the tower shows the typically Belgian intermingling of Gothic and Baroque. The interior is surprisingly light and spacious, with a harmony of colour and form. It has beautiful brick vaulting and particularly impressive, among its rich furnishings, are the carved pulpit (1757) by the Mechelen sculptor Parent and the many tombstones and paintings, including seven by the Brussels painter Th. van Loon (1581–1667) that have recently been restored.

The Pachéco Hospice in a quiet square just north of the church is a famous old people's home founded in 1713 (building early 19th c.). Near by in the Rue de Laeken is the Flemish Theatre (Koninklijk Vlaamse Schouwburg or Théâtre Royal Flamand; 1887).

Pachéco Hospice
Flemish Theatre

---

*Saint-Michel (Cathédrale Saint-Michel; St Michael's Cathedral)   C4

The Cathedral of St Michael, still known by the locals as St-Michel et Ste-Gudule, stands majestically on the slope between uptown and downtown Brussels, its impressive façade flanked by two truncated towers. The massive building, once white, is in the simple Brabant-Gothic style and has a broad flight of steps leading up to it.

The Carolingian baptistery that used to stand on this site was dedicated to the Archangel Michael, patron saint of Brussels. In 1047, however, when a Collège, a women's religious community, was founded here it acquired the much-revered relics of St Gudula (d. 712) that had formerly been held by the descendants of King Pépin. For centuries the two saints, St Michael and St Gudula, were the joint patrons of the collegiate church which in the 15th c. was to become the country's State church.

This is where all the country's great official religious occasions have taken place from the time of Duke Philip the Good of Burgundy through the Emperor Charles V, Governors-General Albert and Isabelle and Napoleon right up to the present day. When the church became the seat of the Archbishop of Brussels-Mechelen in 1962 it acquired the status of a cathedral. The present building was begun in the early 13th c. and completed towards the end of the 15th c. Its stylistic elements range from the transition from Romanesque to Gothic (in the choir and ambulatory) through Early and High Gothic (in the choir and aisles) to Late Gothic (towers).

Location
Place Ste-Gudule

Metro station
Gare Centrale

Buses
29, 38, 63, 65, 71

The cathedral's rather sombre interior gives the effect of harmonious spaciousness, the most impressive feature being the 16 unique stained-glass windows. The greater part of the 1200 panes, like those by Bernaert von Orley in the transept, date from the 16th c.

Besides the stained glass the many sculptures and paintings, and L. Delmotte's lovely wrought-iron screens (18th c.) are very striking.

SS Michael and Gudula are everywhere to be seen – in statues, paintings and stained-glass windows.

Interior

Saint-Michel

Another oft-repeated theme is the legend of the Miracle of the Blessed Sacrament when Jews were alleged, in 1370, to have stolen and stabbed the consecrated Host, causing blood to flow from the punctured wound. As a result four unfortunate Jewish families were condemned to be burnt at the stake. Although unsupported by any hard evidence the legend survived for centuries and is reflected in numerous works of art in the church. In 1968 the legend was acknowledged to be false and unjust and a bronze plaque in the Chapel of the Blessed Sacrament (see below) warns of the tendentious nature of the accusations.

Choir

The most impressive part of the church is the choir (1215–65), its triforium (1273) especially enchanting when it is illuminated.
To the left and right of the High Altar (late 19th c.) are the tombs of Duke John of Brabant and his wife Margaret of York (d. 1312 and 1322 respectively) and of the Archduke Ernest of Austria (d. 1595), Governor-General of the Netherlands and brother of Emperor Rudolph II. The choir-stalls come from the former Benedictine Abbey of Forest (see St-Denis à Forest).
Six splendid tapestries by Van der Borght (17th c.), that seem to have been inspired by Rubens, are hung in the choir at certain times, particularly in July and August. They depict various episodes from the legend of the Miracle of the Blessed Sacrament (cf. above).
The central three windows in the choir were made by the Court stained-glass artist Nikolaus Rombouts in 1525, while the outer two, in the same style, date from 1550. They depict characters from the history of the Netherlands.

Chapelle de la Madeleine

Behind the choir is the Magdalen Chapel (1282; renovated in the Baroque Style in 1675), with an Italian alabaster altar dated 1538 from the Abbaye de la Cambre (see entry), a charming bust of the Madonna and Child, probably by Konrad Meyt (16th c.) and 19th c. stained glass in the Gothic Transitional style with scenes from the Bible and Church history.

Ambulatory

In the ambulatory (13th c.), on the right, is a statue of the Virgin by Artus Quellinus the Elder (1645) and a noteworthy sculpture of the 16th c. Brabant school ("Holy Sepulchre and Resurrection").
On the left, near the Chapel of the Blessed Sacrament, is a plaque commemorating the city painter Rogier van der Weyden (1400–61) who is buried here (see Famous People), and a statue of the great Flemish mystic Jan Ruysbroeck (d. 1381).

Chapelle du Saint-
Sacrement

The Chapelle du St-Sacrement (Chapel of the Blessed Sacrament – 1534–39) contains a row of 16th c. windows presented by Charles V and his family in honour of the Blessed Sacrament, with likenesses of the donors and scenes from the history of the alleged Miracle (in the top half of the windows). The first three (from left to right) are based on designs by Bernaert van Orley (1490–1541); the fourth window, which was lost, and the fifth were replaced in 1848 by J.-B. Carponnier, who also created the sixth window.
Below the alabaster altar (19th c.) are the tombs of the

The Cathedral of St Michael, linking uptown and downtown Brussels ▶

Governors-General Albert and Isabelle (d. 1671 and 1633 respectively) whose portraits, copies of works by Peter Paul Rubens, hang on the wall on the left.

Chamber concerts are held in the Chapel, usually in August.

Chapelle de Notre-Dame de la Délivrance

To the right of the choir is the Chapel of Our Lady of the Redemption (Notre-Dame de la délivrance), built 1649–55 in the Gothic style, with beautiful 17th c. stained-glass windows designed by Th. Van Thulden, a pupil of Rubens.

With their dark colours and Baroque architectural background they stand out clearly from the 16th c. stained glass. They depict the benefactors of the Church with their patron saints and, above, episodes from the life of the Virgin.

The Chapel contains several fine tombs, including an outstanding work by the Belgian sculptor Wilhelm Geef (Tomb of Count Friedrich von Merode; 1835), as well as several notable 17th c. paintings.

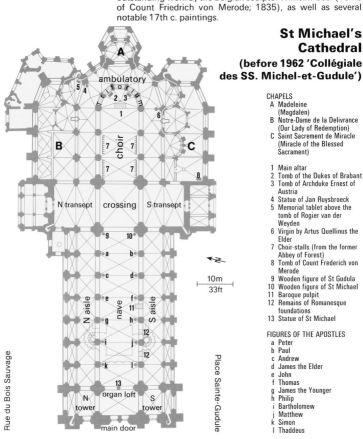

St Michael's Cathedral
(before 1962 'Collégiale des SS. Michel-et-Gudule')

CHAPELS
A Madeleine (Magdalen)
B Notre-Dame de la Delivrance (Our Lady of Redemption)
C Saint Sacrement de Miracle (Miracle of the Blessed Sacrament)

1   Main altar
2   Tomb of the Dukes of Brabant
3   Tomb of Archduke Ernest of Austria
4   Statue of Jan Ruysbroeck
5   Memorial tablet above the tomb of Rogier van der Weyden
6   Virgin by Artus Quellinus the Elder
7   Choir-stalls (from the former Abbey of Forest)
8   Tomb of Count Frederich von Merode
9   Wooden figure of St Gudula
10 Wooden figure of St Michael
11 Baroque pulpit
12 Remains of Romanesque foundations
13 Statue of St Michael

FIGURES OF THE APOSTLES
a Peter
b Paul
c Andrew
d James the Elder
e John
f Thomas
g James the Younger
h Philip
i Bartholomew
j Matthew
k Simon
l Thaddeus

Magnificent stained glass in St Michael's Cathedral ▶

Concert in Saint-Michel

Detail of the pulpit in St Michael's Cathedral

The columns in the 14th–15th c. nave are formed by 12 life-size figures of the Apostles (17th c.). Some of them are by Luc Faid'Herbe (Simon, James the Elder and possibly also John) and Jérôme Duquesnoy the Younger (Paul, Bartholomew, Thomas and Judas Thaddeus).

Nave

The splendid pulpit carved by Hendrik Verbruggen (1669) shows Adam and Eve being expelled from Eden and is a superb example of Belgian Baroque. The flanking semi-spiral staircases were added in 1708 (carvings by van der Haeghen).

Remains of the foundations of a 12th c. Romanesque porch were discovered in 1937 in the floor between the pulpit and the organ loft.

The magnificent windows in the late 13th – early 14th c. south transept and the 14th c. north transept were designed by Bernaert van Orley in the 16th c.

Aisles

The first represents Emperor Charles V, the donor, and his wife Isabella of Portugal kneeling before the shrine of the Miracle of the Blessed Sacrament, with their patrons Charlemagne and St Elizabeth; the second shows the donor of the picture, Queen Maria of Hungary, sister of Charles V and Regent of the Netherlands, kneeling with her husband, King Louis II of Hungary, in front of the Holy Trinity, with their patron saints St Louis and the Virgin Mary.

All the other stained glass in the aisles was made by J.-B. Carponnier in the second half of the 19th c. to designs by Ch. De Groux. They depict scenes from the tale of the Miracle of the Blessed Sacrament. Of particular interest are the first two windows in the south aisle (next to the transept) with the coats of arms of the Royal Families of Saxe-Coburg and Orléans and of the Kingdom of Belgium and the House of Habsburg, gifts from the Belgian Kings Leopold I and Leopold II in memory of their wives Louise-Marie and Marie-Henriette.

Saint-Nicholas (church)   C3

The little Church of Saint Nicholas near the Grand'Place (see entry) is one of the most appealing churches in Brussels. It has had a turbulent history. According to the plaque just inside the church it was closely linked with Brussels becoming a city. It was originally built by the merchants during the Romanesque period (11th–12th c.) as a market church in honour of their patron saint, then renovated in the Gothic style in the 14th–15th c. and rebuilt both after its destruction in the 16th c. during the Wars of Religion and after the bombardment of 1695 (see Grand'Place). Only the tower, that over the centuries had either collapsed or burned down three times, was not rebuilt.

The interior exudes a warm, welcoming atmosphere and is richly furnished with wood-panelled walls, Classicist High Altar, carved wooden confessionals and pulpit and a lovely wrought-iron choir screen (all 18th c.).

On the left side altar is a 15th c. Madonna and on the right-hand choir pillar is a Spanish figure of Christ (16th c.). In front of the pulpit is the copper Shrine of the Martyrs of Gorcum (1868), in memory of those who in 1572 were horribly tortured and then executed in Brielle (near Rotterdam) after it had fallen to the Geuze. The church also contains several interesting paintings.

Location
Rue de Tabora, on the corner of Petite Rue au Beurre

Metro station
Bourse

Buses
34, 48, 95, 96

Trams
52, 55, 58, 62, 81

Opening times
Daily 10–midday and 4–6 p.m.

Sainte-Catherine

Surroundings

There are shops on either side of the church, some of them consisting of only two rooms one on top of the other, giving the church a rather raffish appearance.
A short distance to the north are the Passage St-Honoré and the Galerie du Centre which, together with the Galerie Rivoli, form an attractive shopping centre.

Sainte-Catherine (church)   C3

Location
Place Ste-Catherine

Metro station
Ste-Catherine

The Church of St Catherine, in a densely populated district west of the Inner Boulevards, is a majestic building that lends a rather formal note to the commercial area around it.
It was built from 1850 onwards by Joseph Poelaert (see Notre-Dame de Laeken and Palais de Justice) in a mixture of Romantic, Gothic and Renaissance styles to replace the former Church of St Catherine (14th–15th c.; enlarged late 16th c.) which became a ruin about 1800. The tower of the old building is, surprisingly, still standing and though not joined to the new church serves as its bell-tower.
The interior is filled with valuable old works of art. In the left aisle is the Vierge Noire (Black Madonna; 14th or 15th c.). a statue of Mary carved from light-coloured stone which presumably turned black when it stood in the medieval church, and was affected by the damp from the Senne which used to flow near by and was used for carrying peat. On the right-hand side altar is a painting by G. de Crayer (1584–1669) of the Glorification of St Catherine. The sacristy behind the altar

A view of the Church of St Catherine

(currently accessible only during services, 8 a.m. and 6.30 p.m.) contains fine examples of the craft of the goldsmith as well as interesting paintings.

The 11th–12th c. Tour Noire (Black Tower) in the Place du Samedi behind the church was once part of Brussels' first city wall. It was restored in 1895.

Tour Noire

West of the church, on the site of a former wharf, is the charming old Fish Market (Vieux Marché-aux-Poissons, between Quai aux Briques (Brick Quay) and Quai au Bois à Brûler (Firewood Quay)), with its many fishmongers and seafood restaurants. Its water-troughs have recently been restored to it and it is now the site of the Anspach Fountain (Fontaine d'Anspach, 1897) which once stood in the Place de Brouckère (see Boulevards du Centre).

Fish Market

Sainte-Marie

See Boulevards

*Saints Pierre et Guidon à Anderlecht (church)   D1

The Collegiate Church of SS-Pierre et Guidon, whose lovely spire catches the eye from quite a distance, is a remarkable 14th–16th c. Gothic building erected on 11th c. foundations.

Location
Place de la Vaillance
(Anderlecht)

The Collegiate Church of SS-Pierre et Guidon in Anderlecht

Tervuren

<table>
<tr><td>Metro station
St-Guidon

Buses
46, 49, LN</td><td>Together with the nearby Erasmus House (see Maison d'Erasme) and Anderlecht's Beguine Convent it forms part of a particularly valuable culturally significant complex. The oldest parts of the church date back to 1350 and its interior is distinguished by a series of medieval wall-paintings which merit closer inspection.
Some are well preserved and were restored in the late 19th c. The splendid Triumphal Arch of Christ (14th c.), the statue of St Catherine (14th–15th c.) and some notable paintings, including an "Adoration of the Magi". are also worth seeing.</td></tr>
<tr><td>Crypt</td><td>Below the choir, which dates from about 1470 after the demolition of the Romanesque part of the building, is a very interesting five-aisled crypt, built in the late 11th c. presumably as a church above ground level. It contains the stone coffin of St Guido, the patron saint of horses (pilgrimages with the blessing of horses on Whit Monday and the first Sunday after 12 September).
The church tower was begun at the beginning of the 16th c. but not completed until 1898 (designed by the architect van Ysendyck).</td></tr>
<tr><td>Beguine Convent</td><td>Near the church (4 Rue du Chapelain) are the remains of the Beguine Convent of Anderlecht (Vieux Béguinage d'Anderlecht), founded in 1252, with a small folk museum.</td></tr>
</table>

Tervuren

See Musée Royal de l'Afrique Centrale

*Théâtre Royal de la Monnaie (Opéra National; National Opera House) C3

<table>
<tr><td>Location
Place de la Monnaie

Metro station
De Brouckère

Buses
29, 63, 65, 66, 71

Trams
52, 55, 58, 62, 81, 90</td><td>The Thèâtre Royal de la Monnaie was elevated to the rank of National Opera House (Opéra National) in 1963. It is right in the city centre in the Place de la Monnaie, near the Place de Brouckère.
The building owes its name to the 15th c. Hôtel de la Monnaie (Mint) of the Dukedom of Brabant which stood on the site of the present-day square. The Mint was demolished in 1531 and replaced by a square. The first theatre was erected in 1698 by the Governor-General of the Netherlands, Jean-Paul Bombarda. It could seat 1200 but was initially not very successful. A radical conversion was decided on in 1810 and the new building was opened in May 1819. The architect, Damesme, created a theatre in the Neo-Classic style surrounded by a roofed arcade. The eight Ionic columns of the façade are topped by a triangular pediment containing a bas-relief celebrating the Harmony of human Passions.
The theatre faces the busy Place de la Monnaie, today a pedestrian precinct with fountains, benches and islands of greenery. On the west side of the square towers the Centre Monnaie with its shopping arcades, post office and city council offices. The site of the Centre Monnaie was occupied up until 1965 by the 19th c. Hôtel des Postes (main post office) which was demolished when the area between the Place de la Monnaie and the Place de Brouckère was modernised.</td></tr>
</table>

Théâtre Royal de la Monnaie, Brussels' National Opera House

The square was already a popular meeting-place for the people of 19th c. and *fin-de-siècle* Brussels. Theatre performances began at five in the evening and lasted until 9 p.m. and the audiences would finish the evening off in the nearby establishments which were just starting to be gaslit – a sensation for those days. This is where toasts were drunk to the stars of the day whose names were on everyone's lips – Mademoiselle Mars, Mademoiselle Duchesnois, La Malibran. The bust of the actor F. J. Talma was displayed in the huge foyer.

On 31 January 1855 the theatre burned down and only the columns and the bas-relief survived unscathed. The architect Poelaert rebuilt it in a year and the auditorium was enlarged at the expense of the outer gallery. The new theatre was opened by King Leopold I and it was thenceforth restricted to opera and ballet.

The theatre was connected with a crucial event in Belgium's history which centred on Daniel François Auber's opera "Portici" which was premièred at the theatre during the Dutch rule of Belgium in 1829. Having been withdrawn from the repertoire for a time because of the unrest in the city, it was subsequently played again on 25 August 1830 and the public attended this second première en masse. On hearing the aria "Amour sacré de la Patrie" (Sacred love of the Fatherland), sung by Lafeuillade Mazaniello, the crowd rushed out, as the hero bellowed "To arms", to the houses where the Dutch live, and then on to the Parc de Bruxelles, thus sparking off the revolution that was to give Belgium its independence.

The Brussels Opera is firmly established as one of the best opera-houses in Europe. It has been the scene of many glittering world premières and for over 20 years has been the home of the famous Ballet of the 20th Century under its exceptional choreographer, Maurice Béjart.

The Opera House is currently being renovated at great expense.

Théâtre Royal du Parc

See Palais Royal

*Toone's Puppet Theatre (Théâtre et Musée de Toone VII)   C3

Location
6 Impasse Schuddeveld

Metro station
Gare Centrale

Buses
29, 34, 48, 63, 65, 66, 71,
95, 96

Box office
tel. 5117137, 5135486

Opening times
daily from midday

Barely a hundred yards from the Grand'Place (see entry) is the narrow pedestrian Rue des Bouchers (Street of the Butchers). Every building there and in the Rue Grétry farther up houses a restaurant, café or revue bar. The air reeks of beer, "moules et frites", chicken, spaghetti and kebabs. Turning into a side street, the Petite Rue des Bouchers, the visitor is soon standing in front of a little cul-de-sac that used to be called "'s cudde velt", the meadow where the cattle graze. This was the site of one of the city's first slaughterhouses. Houses were gradually built up round it, crowding in on the narrow alleyway that later came to be called Impasse Schuddeveld as a reminder of its past.

At the end of this well-lit cul-de-sac, engraved in the white stone arch above the little doorway, is the single word: TOONE. Like a roguish wink it invites the visitor to cross the threshold of a crooked house, built in 1696 on the site of a wooden house destroyed by Marshal de Villeroy's bombardment in 1695. This is where, nearly three centuries later, José Géal, the seventh in the Toone dynasty, set up his theatre in 1966.

Interior

Can this be a theatre? Entering the door, you find yourself in a tiny corridor. Don't bump into the lovely old pianola. It still works: if you put in a 5-franc piece it plays an old street-organ tune as you go into the bar. Here, amidst a colourful audience and the swirling blue tobacco smoke, you can breathe in history: a wooden-beamed ceiling with the bar still clinging to it, a genuine Gothic fireplace, little oak tables, benches and chairs, a bar. An old staircase leads to the upper floor. On the walls hang plaques, photographs, drawings and one or two puppets.

Auditorium

Through an open door you catch a glimpse of the next room, the auditorium: rows of benches facing the stage, with small blue, red, green or yellow cushions. The numbers of the seats are chalked on the floor, which slopes gently towards the stage. It is a real theatre stage but in miniature to suit the size of the puppets that play on it.

In the wall to the right of the stage is a circle of light. What's it for? Wait and see! Three dull thuds: in the circle appears the head of José Géal, Toone VII, wearing a jaunty cap. And now a festival of laughter begins: the adventures of people with wooden heads, dressed like early 20th c. *bons vivants*, or like musketeers, noblemen of the past or à la mode. Their immobile faces are etched with the expression of every character they portray. Their voice is that of Toone. From time to time a glance at the light circle: Toone VII, José Géal, comedian, tragedian, singer, strolling player, poet, arranger, chronicler, producer, he changes the voice and the expression, he is talking and singing at the same time as his puppets.

What piece are these wooden artistes performing? "The farce of death, that had almost died out" by Michel de Ghelderode.
To begin with, however, they used to do the Passion play as it was performed long, long ago in the cellars of the Marolles (see Les Marolles). An amazing Passion play with Judas Iscariot playing the Fool. Then the repertoire was enlarged to include the Knights Templar, the heroes of Alexandre Dumas, Victor Hugo, Michel Zevaco, William Shakespeare, Paul Féval, Henri Conscience and of course Michel de Ghelderode. Often, too, there were improvisations, inspired by famous periods in the history of the Marolles.
And all this in this unusual dialect when you cannot tell whether there are more French words than Flemish, or vice versa.

Repertoire

This dialect gradually evolved a long time ago in the quarter of Brussels known as Les Marolles (see entry), which was lived in at one time by the nobility and the middle classes. French nuns had their convent here. The city's gallows loomed not far away. This was the quarter that Pieter Bruegel chose as the scene for his "Crucifixion"; this is where Andreas Vesalius, the inventor of modern surgery, secretly obtained by night the corpses he needed for his work. But this was also where Walloon and Flemish workers mixed, talking to one another in a bizarre kind of French, liberally sprinkled with Flemish with the odd word of Spanish picked up from the soldiers of the Duka of Alba: this was how this odd, racy Marolle dialect came into being.

Marolle dialect

And there finally is where it all began, one day in 1830, with the appearance of an enigmatic character by the name of Toone, derived no doubt from "Anton", with his small world of versatile puppets.
This first Toone, nicknamed the Elder, undoubtedly had his predecessors but none attained his degree of fame. Toone I became the founder of a real dynasty.
Into his world of puppets he introduced a strange Master of Ceremonies: Woltje, the little Walloon, who crops up in all the Toone dynasties. In his checked jacket, his dirty cap at a jaunty angle, doffed in greeting, he personifies the "Ketje", the Brussels street urchin.
Since Woltje spoke Marolle dialect all the other puppets had to speak it too. From then on Toone's language was Woltje's. Toone I reigned from 1835 to 1880 in the cellars of the Marolles, his subterranean palaces. He nominated as his successor Franz Taelemans, Toone II, who was known as the Ancestor.
After his death in 1890, Toone III, who came from Germany, began to perform plays about knights in armour until he hanged himself in 1911 among his puppets. He was replaced by a pupil of Toone I, Toone IV, who performed for 15 years before abdicating in favour of his assistant Daniel de Ladewyck, who reigned as Toone V until 1935.
For two years Toone's theatre slumbered until Pierre Welleman revived it in 1937. He became Toone VI. His theatre was often the target of the city planners and fell prey to their axe. And just

Toone dynasty

before Easter 1963, as he was about to give his first performance in a downtown café where he thought he had finally found a home, he fell foul of persecution by the planners once again. Toone VI's first performance there was also his last, and was in fact also given by his principal assistant. This man, besides being a puppet-maker, had also been the Director of the Children's Theatre since 1954 and had, since 1962, been a member of the Presidium of the International Puppet Union, a body recognised by UNESCO. He was also the creator of a famous children's television programme: "Bonhommet et Tilapin". His name was José Géal. Toone's theatre appeared to be condemned to death – but Toone, they say, is immortal.

Toone VII

At the end of 1963 José Géal was crowned Toone VII. He was then 32 years old. Under his rule the Brussels Puppet Theatre was revived and regained its audience, that of the adult who is a child at heart.
In 1966 he bought the old house, after it had been officially restored, in Schuddeveld Alley where the tower of the Town Hall in the Grand'Place (see entry) still casts its long shadow.

*Waterloo

Location
18 km (11 miles) S of
Brussels

Bus
W (from Gare du Midi)

The village of Waterloo (pop. 6000), in the province of Brabant, 18 km (11 miles) south of Brussels, is known throughout the world as the site of the Battle of Waterloo in 1815.
The battle that on 18 June 1815 was to decide the fate not only of France but of all of Europe was called "The Battle of Waterloo" by Wellington, who commanded the English forces, because that was where he had his headquarters. Blücher called it the "Battle of Belle-Alliance" because that was the name of the farm where the two of them met after their victory. After his victory over the Prussian troops at Ligny (16 June) Napoleon turned to face the main force of the English and Hanoverians under Wellington; however Geisenau, Blücher's Chief of General Staff, turned the retreat into an attack on the French flanks and relieved Wellington's troops, who had already begun to fall back, thus enabling Wellington to issue his report of victory that evening in Waterloo.
The church, a prominent landmark, dates from 1855 and has many inscriptions inside commemorating the English who fell in 1815.

Monuments

There are three monuments at the crossroads of the broad Charleroi road and the old Ohain defile which did so much damage to Napoleon's troops – it is now wider and paved. The first on the left is a stone column with bronze flags. This is the monument to the Belgians and its inscription reads "To the Belgians who fell on 18 June 1815 fighting to defend the flag and the honour of the armies."
On the far side of the crossroads, still on the left, is the monument to the Hanoverians, surrounded by a grille. At the back is the inscription "In memory of their comrades-at-arms who died in glory on 18 June 1815."
Opposite, on the other side of the road, stands the English monument commemorating Lieutenant Colonel Gordon, Wellington's Adjutant, who fell on this spot.

Centre of Waterloo: Butte du Lion (Lion Mound) ▶

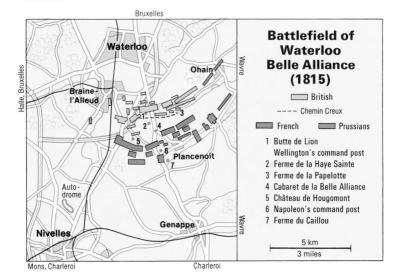

These last two monuments indicate the original level of the site. The surrounding earth was removed and used to make the Lion Mound.

Butte du Lion (Lion Mound)

The road from the monuments to the Lion Mound is the former Ohain defile. The mound stands within the town of Braine-l'Alleud where the Prince of Orange, who commanded the Dutch-Belgian troops, was wounded. In 1816 he married the Grand Duchess Anna, sister of the Tsar Alexander, and when his father abdicated in 1840 he became King William II of the Netherlands. He died in 1849.

The lion, whose right forepaw rests on a globe, stands on a stone column that reaches right down to the foot of the mound. The cone-shaped mound of earth round the column comes from the field of battle and was painstakingly collected by men and women in baskets. The monument was paid for by the Allies but has been maintained by the Belgian Government since 1830. The Lion is the work of the Prince of Orange's sculptor, Arthur-Louis van Geel. Its base is 7 m (23 ft) high and the lion itself is 1·5 m (5 ft) high and 4·45 m (14·6 ft) long. It weighs 28 tons. The mound consists of 32,000 cu. m (1,129,920 cu. ft) of earth, is 45 m (148 ft) high and has a circumference of 500 m (547 yd). It covers 2 ha (5 acres) and there are 226 steps leading up to the top. The enormous quantity of earth needed to build the mound was taken from the east side, resulting in the unfortunate disappearance of the Ohain defile. The base of the monument bears only one inscription, 'XVIII June, MDCCCXV'.

Rotunda

At the base of the mound is a rotunda containing the panorama of the Battle of Waterloo by the French military artist Louis Dumoulin.

At the foot of the Butte du Lion: a rotunda with the panorama . . .

. . . of the Battle of Waterloo by the military artist Louis Dumoulin

World Trade Centre (WTC)

Location
W of the North Station

Metro station
Gare du Nord

The first tower blocks of the World Trade Centre (WTC) rear up into the sky west of the Gare du Nord (North Station). Building began as long ago as 1968, when over 13,000 people had to leave their homes. When the work is finally completed the 53 ha (131 acre) site should have eight tower blocks, each of over 30 storeys, mainly intended for all kinds of service companies. Various shops, licensed premises and cultural facilities make for a relaxed atmosphere in the buildings that have already been erected.

SWIFT

WTC Tower 1 contains the head offices of the Society for Worldwide Interbank Financial Telecommunications (SWIFT).

Practical Information

Airlines

British Airways
Centre International Rogier, 9th floor, tel. 219 42 20

PanAm
Department Avianca, 5 Rue de Loxom, tel. 751 81 95

TWA
5, Boulevard de l'Empereur, tel. 513 79 15

South African Airlines
1303 Centre International Rogier B 224, tel. 218 48 00

Qantas
66 Avenue Louise, tel. 513 27 92

Air Canada
66 Boulevard de l'Impératrice, tel. 513 62 10

Airport

Brussels National Airport is located at Zaventem, about 14 km
(9 miles) from the city centre, and has its own rail service into
and out of the city. (Motorists should follow the signs to
Zaventem.)

Trains leave from Brussels Central or Brussels North every 20
minutes, starting at 6.30 a.m. (Brussels Central). The journey
takes 30 minutes.

Transfer by rail

For information about flights, the telephone number to ring is
511 90 30 (SABENA – Belgian National Airline).
For information about landing times, the telephone number to
ring is 720 71 67

Information

Antiques

The quarter for antique-dealers is around the Place du Grand-
Sablon, where the antique market is held from 10 a.m. to 1 p.m.
on Saturdays (see Markets).
The well-known art-dealers are to be found on the Avenue
Louise and Boulevard de Waterloo, while antique-dealers and
second-hand shops are more likely to be in the Chaussée
d'Ixelles and Chaussée de Wavre.

Breakdown services

See Driving

One of Brussels' many cafés

Cafés

Cafés are very numerous in Brussels, especially along the Inner Boulevards, around the Opera house, the Stock Exchange and the Porte Namur.
Belgian cafés are more like pubs or bars, where you can go for a drink, than cafés in the English sense. If what you want is a light meal or a cup of tea, it is better to look for a cafeteria or a Tea-room, or salon de thé, which also serve coffee and cakes.

Calendar of events

January	Ideal Home Exhibition (Salon de la Maison Idéale) Motor Show (Salon de l'Auto; every 2 years)
February	Holiday Fair (Salon des Vacances) Antiques Fair (Foire des Antiquaires)
March–April	Feast of the "Fat Ox" Book Fair
April–May	Cherryblossom-time in Boitsfort Public viewing of the Royal greenhouses at Laeken Concours Reine Elisabeth (musical competition) Brussels Trade Fair (Foire Commerciale de Bruxelles) Son et lumière in the Grand'Place

The Brussels Marathon (20 km (12½ miles)). June

Ommegang (1st Thurs.): Brussels Carnival and, since the 14th c., the most magnificent spectacle of the Brussels year. July
Originally, the religious procession of Notre-Dame-à-la-Branche (Our Blessed Lady, om't Stokske), the ranks of this famous procession were swollen over the years by the civilian and military dignitaries, the craft guilds and the corporations and it rapidly developed into a grand parade which is still remembered hundreds of years later.
The present Ommegang, which processes through the Grand'Place on the first Thursday in July, is a historical revival of the festivities staged by the Governor of Brussels on 2 June 1549 in honour of Emperor Charles V, his eldest son Phillip, then Duke of Brabant, and his sisters Eleonore, Queen of France, and Marie, Queen of Hungary.
The presence of local worthies and members of the Belgian nobility add to the success of the Ommegang. Fur-trimmed costumes, caparisoned horses, plumed headgear, twirling banners, acrobats and stilt-walkers go to make up a marvellous spectacle in the incomparable setting of that most magnificent of stages: the Grand'Place: the Ommegang fully lives up to the pageantry of yesteryear and draws countless visitors every year.

Belgian National Holiday with big street parties and firework displays. 21 July

21 July–about 20 August: Brussels Fair (Foire du Midi). July/August
This grand annual fair around the Gare du Midi (South Station) was first held on the Boulevard du Midi in 1885. As early as 1882 several showmen had already successfully set up their booths at the foot of the Porte de Hal and today the fair, which operates from 21 July until about 20 August, extends from the Porte de Hal to the Porte d'Anderlecht, a distance of about 2 km (1¼ miles).
Magic castles, fortune-tellers, mirror-images, Ferris wheels, merry-go-rounds, and other fairground attractions crowd in upon booths selling "caricolles" (snails), chips by the bag, dried herring, grilled "boudin" and black pudding, hot dogs, langoustines and the famous "smoutebollen" (a kind of doughnut). A taste of these delicacies, washed down by a hearty "gueuze" or "kriek", plunges visitors right into the very special atmosphere that this fair has generated for many, many years.

Raising of the "Meiboom": the history of the "meiboom" (maypole) goes back about 700 years to when a wedding-party from Brussels was attacked by folk from Leuven but came off unscathed thanks to the intervention of the Crossbowmen's Guild, the Compagnos de Saint-Laurent. Ever since, as a token of gratitude, this guild has enjoyed the privilege of planting a tree (white beech) on the corner of the Rue des Sables and the Rue du Marait every year on 9 August. The folk from Leuven naturally still keep on trying to get their own back by stealing this symbolic tree. Planting the maypole is probably one of the most treasured pieces of Brussels folklore. 9 August
Bands, guilds and the Brussels giants – Jantje, Mieke, Jeffke and Rooske – combine on this occasion to make up a merry procession. Good cheer is the order of the day, with the beer flowing freely and the air heavy with the smell of tasty hot dogs.
Opening of the Royal Palace
Yvo-Van-Damme Memorial

Practical Information

"Holy Island" festival and Bruegel festivities. The city's "holy island" (Ilot sacré), the quarter bordering the Grand'Place, with its maze of narrow lanes crowded with numerous restaurants and typical pubs can certainly conjure up everything but sadness. Here can be found mimes, painters and artists, jugglers, hippies and intellectuals in a relaxed atmosphere unmatched anywhere else in Brussels. The local traders have set up a "free community" with its own mayor and council.

In September every year, during the Bruegel festivities, this part of Brussels is brimming with atmosphere, helped along by the appetising smells of the local dishes that should be accompanied by several jugs of delicious "cambrinus".

Europalia (every 2 years)

October

Food and Good Housekeeping exhibition (Salon d'alimentation et des arts ménagers).

December

International Show-jumping (Jumping International de Bruxelles).

Christmas: Cribs, Christmas decorations. Christmas is celebrated in Belgium, as in France, as a festive season for good food and good cheer. The children get presents from St Nicholas (5 December) but the run-up to this begins back in October and the Christmas decorations go up in the streets and department stores many weeks before Christmas itself.

Camp sites

Huizingen
6 Provinciaal Domein, tel. 356 54 03

Beersel
75 Ukkelseweg, tel. 376 25 61

Grimbergen
64 Veldkantstraat, tel. 269 25 97

Ohain
Renipont, 7a Ry-Beau-Ry, tel. 653 66 77

Car hire

Some addresses

Avis
Place Rogier, tel. 354 07 59

Europcar
Station Bruxelles Midi, 33 Place Bara, tel. 648 00 74

Hertz
8 Boulevard M. Lemonnier, tel. 513 28 86

Interrent
233 Avenue Louise, tel. 640 94 00

Car parks

Albertine, 10 Place de la Justice, 5 Rue des Sols
Botanique, 29 Boulevard du Jardin Botanique
Central, 12 Rue de la Madeleine
City, 7 Boulevard Pachéco
City 2, corner of Rue de la Blanchisserie/Rue du Damier
Ecuyer, 11 Rue de l'Ecuyer
Europa, 2 Place du Nouveau Marché-aux-Grains
Flandre, 60 Rue de Flandre
Galeries Ixelles Auto, 23 Chaussée de Wavre
Hilton, 38 Boulevard de Waterloo
Industrie, 26 Rue de l'Industrie
Jamar, 19 Boulevard Jamar
Loi, 25 Avenue des Arts
Louise, 7 Rue de Livourne, 40 Chaussée de Charleroi
Madou, 7 Chaussée de Louvain
Manhattan, Manhattan Center, 19 Rue des Croisades
Monnaie, Rue Fossé-aux-Loups (opposite the Rue Neuve)
Passage 44, 16 Rue de l'Ommegang
Philips, 2 Place de Brouckère
Pont-Neuf, 54 Rue du Pont-Neuf
Putterie Garage, 1 Rue de la Montagne
Rogier, Centre International Rogier, 68 Rue du Progres
Royal Windsor, 5–7 Rue Duquesnoy
Saint-Sauveur, Rue Montagne-aux-Herbes-Potageres
Tour du Midi, 3 Boulevard de l'Europe
World Trade Center, Ilot un, Boulevard E. Jacqmain

Supervised multi-storey car parks (selection)

Chambers of Commerce

The Brussels Chamber of Commerce
500 Avenue Louise, tel. 648 50 02

The U.E.B./V.O.B. (Association of Brussels Enterprises)
75 Rue Botanique, tel. 219 32 23

The Federation of Belgian Chambers of Commerce Abroad
Rue des Sols, tel. 512 26 33

Concerts

See Theatres and concert halls

Conference information

Since Brussels is the headquarters of both NATO and the European Community, it is the permanent home of about 20,000 diplomats and senior officials from all over the world, and has three diplomatic corps. They are accredited to the Court of His Majesty King Baudouin I, to the European Community and, finally, to NATO. About 500 international associations are based here and over 1200 multi-national corporations have made this city their European headquarters. One of the three World Trade Centres (trade marts) is in Brussels.

Practical Information

Crossbowmen

Historians are constantly referring to the important part played by the crossbow in the 11th c., but there is no evidence of its actual use in Belgium – or Europe – until the 13th c. This

Spanish Saracen weapon was supposed to have been brought back by the Crusaders. These dashing knights, however, disliked and despised it, but it was used by the civil militia who did not unduly suffer from such scruples. It was first used as a fighting weapon, then later also for competitions.

The old guilds of the Middle Ages considered it a privilege to dedicate a chapel to their chosen patron saint, and the Crossbowmen's Guild has its chapel in the choir of the Church of Notre-Dame du Sablon (see A to Z).

In Brussels there are three crossbowmen's associations keeping up the ancient tradition, with the term "Serment" denoting the corporation of archers and "Grand Serment" being used for the crossbowmen's associations.

Ancien Grand Serment royal et noble des Arbalétriers de Notre-Dame du Sablon
65 Rue de Ruysbroek

Grand Serment royal et de Saint-George des Arbalétriers de Bruxelles
Shooting range: 6 Rue de Six Jetons

Serment Royal Saint-Sebastien des Archers de Bruxelles
(Royal St Sebastian Corporation of Brussels)

The task of protecting the cities from intruders has always fallen to the guilds. This ancient corporation of militiamen was founded in 1381 and has its origins in the Brussels guild of Crossbowmen. It was first founded in its present form in 1468 in the Church of St Géry at the instigation of Charles the Bold.

Currency

Currency Unit: Belgian Franc (Bfr) = 100 centimes.
Bank notes: 50, 100, 500, 1000 and 5000 Bfr.
Coins: 25 and 50 centimes; 1, 5, 10 and 20 Bfr.

Currency

Import and export of local or foreign currency is not subject to any limitations. Euro-cheques, travellers' cheques or credit cards are convenient and widely accepted.

Currency regulations

Customs regulations

Visitors to Belgium are allowed the usual duty-free allowances of alcohol and tobacco, etc. For goods bought in ordinary shops in Britain or another EEC country (i.e. duty and tax paid) the allowances are 300 cigarettes or 150 cigarillos or 75 cigars or 400 g of tobacco; $1\frac{1}{2}$ litres of alcoholic drinks over $38\cdot8\%$ proof or 3 litres of alcoholic drinks not over $38\cdot8\%$ proof or 3 litres of fortified or sparkling wine, plus 4 litres of still table wine; 75 g of perfume; and 375 cc of toilet-water. For goods bought in a duty-free shop, on a ship or on an aircraft the allowances are two-thirds of these amounts (250 g of tobacco).

27 MHz band CBS radios are not permitted in Belgium and may not be temporarily imported either.

Arrival

Practical Information

Departure

The duty-free allowances on return to Britain are the same as those for British visitors to Belgium.

Driving

Drinking and driving

Any driver who is over the alcohol limit of 80 mg (100 ml) runs the risk of losing his licence.

Seat belts

The wearing of seat belts in town and on motorways is compulsory in Belgian-licensed vehicles for both driver and passengers (except on grounds of pregnancy or a serious medical condition).
Foreign visitors have to comply with this law if their vehicles are fitted with seat belts.

Children

Children under 12 are not allowed to sit next to the driver if the vehicle has a seat at the rear.

Speed limits

60 kilometres per hour (37·5 miles per hour) in built-up areas unless there is a road sign to the contrary.
120 kph (75 mph) on motorways and 4-lane highways; 90 kph (56·25 mph) on all other roads outside built-up areas.

Driving licence

Foreign visitors need to have their own national driving licence or an international driving licence.

Studded snow tyres

Studded snow tyres are only permitted when very bad weather conditions make it necessary.
When snow tyres are used they have to be fitted to all four wheels, speed may not exceed 60 kph (37·5 mph) and 90 kph (56·25 mph) on motorways and four-lane highways the speed permitted must be clearly shown on the rear of the vehicle, and the vehicle may not exceed 3·5 tonnes in weight.

Right of way

Drivers must give way to rail traffic, trams, etc. and to road traffic coming from the right except on main roads that are indicated as having priority.

Breakdown services

There are emergency telephones on the Belgian motorways which can also be used to call up the motoring organisations' breakdown services.

Accidents

Ambulance: dial 900
Traffic police: dial 901

Motoring organisations

Royal Automobile Club de Belgique (R.A.C.B.) a.s.b.l.
53 Rue d'Arlon, Ixelles, tel. 230 08 08
Touring Club de Belgique (T.C.B.) a.s.b.l.
44–46 Rue de la Loi, Brussels, tel. 233 22 11

Parking

See Car parks

Weather forecast and road conditions

See entry

Embassies

Australia

51–52 Avenue des Arts, tel. 511 39 97

6 Rue de Loxum, tel. 513 79 40	Canada
19–21 rue Luxembourg, tel. 513 66 33	Eire
47 Boulevard du Régent, tel. 512 10·40	New Zealand
26 Rue de la Loi, tel. 230 68 45	South Africa
(consular department) 32 Rue Joseph II, tel. 217 90 00	United Kingdom
(consular section) 25 Boulevard du Régent tel. 513 38 30	United States of America

Food and Drink

Belgium has always been the country of the gourmet and people enjoying a festive meal or relishing a picnic often figure in paintings of the Flemish Old Masters. The Belgian of today still seizes on any excuse to enjoy a good dinner. The people of Brussels are no exception and also prize their food and drink very highly.
Belgian restaurants, especially those in Brussels, enjoy an excellent reputation. Some of the best ones conceal their proficiency in the culinary arts behind an unassuming façade. In addition to the expensive de luxe establishments there are a great many cheaper places where you can also eat well. Anyone wanting to eat à la carte can find what they are looking for in the host of specialised dishes. Many restaurants specialise in their own particular dishes and apart from the restaurants serving standard international cuisine and those providing typical Belgian fare, there is food on offer from all over the world.
For those who want to eat quickly and cheaply, there are snack bars and "fritures" (chip stalls).

Meat Dishes: Specialities
Flemish carbonnade, lean beef casseroled in beer; smoked ham from the Ardennes; veal kidneys à la liégeoise; potato and apple purée with black pudding or liver sausage.

Game:
hare and rabbit à la flamande, marinated in Gueuze and braised with onions and prunes; pheasant à la brabançonne; fieldfare à la liégeoise.

Poultry:
Brussels cockerel: particularly tender young birds reared near Brussels; Waterzooi: chunks of chicken stewed with leeks, cream and egg yolks; roast goose à la visé: goose just boiled and then roasted.

Fish:
green eels: boiled eel flavoured with green herbs; herring in cream; trout, sole, seafood – mussels, lobsters, crabs, prawns served with a variety of sauces.

Fruit:
hothouse grapes and strawberries available all the year round.

Vegetables:
red cabbage à la flamande; asparagus de Malines; braised endives (chicon/witlof); Brussels sprouts (choux de Bruxelles); Brussels is famous for its "pommes frites" (chips) which are prepared with very special care.

Cheese:
Belgian Gouda (St-Bernard, Hertog van Brabant); Trappist cheese (Maredsous, Orval); Herve; Remoudou; Cassette de Beaumont; cream cheese curd (fromage blanc) with onions, chives or cress and radishes.

Pastries and desserts:
cheesecake; creamed rice; sugar biscuits; rice tart; Brussels waffles with sugar, butter, fresh cream and/or fruit; Liège waffles with caramel syrup.

Sweets:
babeluttes (toffees); pralines (local chocolates).

Drinks

Beers:
Gueuze; Lambic; Kriek; Faro, Trappist, Diester, Louvain; Malmedy; Brussels Ketje; Rodenbach bitter; Aerts or Vieux Temps Specials.
Wines are usually from France or Luxembourg.
Spa is the most common mineral water.

Getting to Brussels

By sea and road

Those travelling to Brussels from Britain by road can cross by ferry or hovercraft from Dover and Folkestone, Hull or Felixstowe (ferry only) to Ostend or Zeebrugge, where they can take the E5 motorway straight to Brussels.
Brussels is on the junction of several European motorways:
– E5 (London)–Ostend–Brussels–Cologne
– E10 Amsterdam–Antwerp–Brussels–Paris
– 10–E40 Antwerp–Brussels–Luxembourg

By rail

There is a direct rail and boat service between London and Brussels via Calais or Ostend. Brussels has three main railway stations: the Gare du Nord (North Station), Gare Centrale (Central Station) and Gare du Midi (South Station) (see Railway stations).
There is also a fast jetfoil service between Dover–Ostend connecting with the London–Brussels trains.

By air

Brussels Airport at Zaventem is 14 km (8·75 miles) from the city centre and has its own rail service in and out of the city (see Airport).
There are numerous daily flights into Brussels from Gatwick and Heathrow, as well as frequent flights from Britain's other main airports. North American travellers can fly direct to Brussels from New York and Atlanta (daily), as well as from Detroit, Chicago, Montreal, etc.

Hotels

The hotels are of the usual international comfort standards. It is highly advisable to book in advance during the peak holiday season. Pleasant accommodation can also be found in the guest-houses (auberges) in the small towns and villages around Brussels.

°Amigo, 1–3 Rue d'Amigo, 194 r.   Category
°Astoria, 103 Rue Royale, 125 r.   ****A
°Hilton, 38 Boulevard de Waterloo, 373 r.
°Hyatt Regency Brussels, 250 Rue Royale, 325 r.
°Jolly Hotel Atlanta, 7 Boulevard Adolphe Max, 244 r.
°Metropole, 31 Place de Brouckère, 410 r.
°Royal Windsor, 5–7 Rue Duquesnoy, 300 r.
Arcade Stephanie, 91–93 Avenue Louise, 142 r.
Bedford, 135 Rue du Midi, 250 r.
Best Western President Centre, 160 Rue Royale, 73 r.
Brussels Europa, 107 Rue de la Loi, 240 r.
Holiday Inn Brussels Airport, 7 Holidaystraat, 288 r.
Mayfair, 381–383 Avenue Louise, 95 r.
Ramada Brussels, 38 Chausée de Charleroi, 202 r.
Brussels Sheraton, 3 Place Rogier, 483 r.

L'Agenda, 6–8 Rue de Florence, 40 r.   ****B
Alfa Louise, 4 Rue Blanche, 50 r.
Arenberg, 15 Rue d'Assaut, 150 r.
Ascot, 1 Place Loix, 60 r.
Auberge de Waterloo, 212 Waterloosesteenweg
Belson, Chaussée de Louvain, 90 r.
Best Western President Nord, 107 Boulevard Adolphe Max, 63 r.
Brussels, 311–319 Avenue Louise, 46 r.
La Cascade, 14 Rue de la Source, 42 r.
Charlemagne, 25–27 Boulevard Charlemagne, 62 r.
County House of Brussels, 2–4 Square des Héros, 120 r.
Delta, 17–21 Chaussée de Charleroi, 260 r.
Diplomat, 32 Rue J. Stas, 70 r.
Etap L.L.N., 61 Avenue de Lauzelle
Euro Flat, 50–62 Boulevard Charlemagne
Forum, 2 Avenue du Haut Pont, 78 r.
Lambermont, 322 Boulevard Lambermont, 45 r.
Mac Donald, 321–325 Avenue Louise
Manos, 100–102 Chaussée de Charleroi, 32 r.
New Siru, 1 Place Rogier, 103 r.
Novotel, Olmenstraat, 160 r.
Palace, 3 Rue Gineste, 360 r.
Park Hotel Yser, 21–22 Avenue de l'Yser, 46 r.
Scheers Grand Hotel, 132 Boulevard Adolphe Max, 62 r.
Sofitel, 15 Bessenfeldstraat, 120 r.

Arcade Sainte-Catherine, Place Ste-Catherine, 230 r.   ***
Armorial, 101 Boulevard Brand Whitlock, 15 r.
Auberge Saint-Michel, 15 Grand'Place
Central, 3 Rue A. Orts, 150 r.
Des Colonies, 6–10 Rue des Croisades, 100 r.
La Concorde Louise, 59 Rue de la Concorde, 26 r.
Du Congrès, 42 Rue du Congres, 38 r.
Derby, 24 Avenue de Tervuren, 30 r.
La Legende, 33 Rue de l'Etuve, 30 r.
Leopold III, 11 Square Joséphine Charlotte, 15 r.
Lloyd George, 12 Avenue Lloyd George, 16 r.
La Madeleine, 22 Rue de la Montagne, 30 r.
Plasky, 212 Avenue Plasky, 30 r.
Queen Anne, 110 Boulevard E. Jacqmain, 57 r.

Jazz

See Nightlife

Language

Brussels is officially bilingual and all the street signs, etc. are in both French and Dutch (Flemish).

In Belgium as a whole the Flemings live in the river basin of the Scheldt and the Walloons in the basin of the Meuse, with a German-speaking minority around Eupen, St-Vith and Arlon. The language frontier between Flanders and Wallonia has hardly changed since the Middle Ages and runs more or less from Visé on the Meuse west, across Waremme, Halle and Ronse to Menin on the French border. North of this line people speak a kind of Dutch, south of it they speak French.

Like Dutch, Flemish is a branch of the Low German language group and in fact only differs from Dutch to the extent that Cockney differs from Geordie in English language terms. Flemish ceased to be used as a written language after the Dutch War of Independence when all Flemish literature was burned by order of the Duke of Alba. It was only under the Dutch administration between 1814 and 1830 that Flemish ceased to be discriminated against. Soon afterwards Dutch was being spoken in the north of Belgium rather than Flemish. After bitter language disputes in the 19th c., Dutch also displaced French which had been the official language of the Flemish area. In the forefront of the Flemish Movement were several well-known 19th and 20th c. writers, among them Felix Timmermans (1886–1947).

Walloon

Walloon, an ancient French dialect with some elements of Celtic and German, has practically died out. It never became important as a written language, French having tended to fulfil this function since the 12th c.

French

French developed from Vulgar Latin after the Roman Occupation of Celtic Gaul. Although it acquired a number of words of Celtic and later also of Germanic origin, it has kept its Romance character. For centuries it was the most important Romance language spoken by the educated élite and in diplomatic circles. The French polite forms are used when speaking to people so that 'Monsieur', 'Madame' or 'Mademoiselle' are added to the end of a phrase and '*s'il vous plaît*' (please) is often added when asking for something.

Leisure parks

Country parks

Hofstade
On the Vilvoorde-Mechelen road; tel. (015) 61 13 01/02
Beach, swimming-pool, boating, walks, roller-skating, sailing.

Huizingen
Between Beersel and Dworp, near Halle; tel. (02) 356 38 03
Camping, open-air swimming-pool, sunbathing areas, boating, mini-golf, outdoor zoo.

Walibi (Wavre-Limal-Bierges)
300 m (328 yd) after the Wavre exit on the Brussels–Namur
motorway, alongside the Wavre-Limette expressway.
A 50 ha (124 acre) theme park offering 30 rides and 5 shows
all within the price of admission – Dolphinarium, Sensorama,
The Secret of the Unicorn (Tintin/Tim), Water Teleski, The
Tornado, plus all the fun of the fair for children and adults. You
need to allow a whole day for a visit.
Open 1 April–30 September 10 a.m.–7 p.m. daily

Park Parmentier   Other leisure parks
19 Avenue Parmentier, Woluwé-Saint-Pierre, tel. (02) 770 22
95 Park Saint-Exupéry, 87 Avenue des Anciens Combattants,
Kraainem, tel. (02) 241 78 34

Markets

The Grand'Place is the venue for a bird and flower market every   Birds, flowers
Sunday morning.

The book and antiques market is held every Saturday from   Antiques, books
9 a.m. to 3 p.m. and every Sunday from 9 a.m. to 1 p.m. in the
Place due Grand-Sablon. The stalls are in green and red, the
Brussels colours.

See A to Z, Flea market   Flea market

The Place Sainte-Catherine in the city centre offers a vast range   Vegetables, fruit
of fruit and vegetables from 8 a.m. to 4 p.m. daily in winter and
up to 6 p.m. in the summer.
The Sunday market next to the Gare du Midi (South Station)
sells textiles of all kinds, as well as exotic and aromatic food
from the Mediterranean.

The horse market takes place from 6 a.m. to 1 p.m. on Fridays   Horses
in the Place de la Duchesse, Anderlecht.

Dogs, cats, rabbits, etc. all go to make up the lively and   Pets
attractive spectacle of the pet market in the Rue Ropsy-
Chaudron on Sunday mornings.

The bicycle market is held on the Boulevard du Midi every   Bicycles
Sunday morning.

Each of the communes in Greater Brussels naturaly has its own   Other markets
local weekly, monthly or annual market in addition to those
described above.

Lost property

SABENA: Lost property office   Plane
Brussels National Airport, arrival concourse tel. 720 91 13
Lost property office of the Belgian Airways Administration:
Brussels Airport National, visitors concourse (1st floor),
weekdays only, tel. 511 18 60

Lost property office, 15 Avenue de la Toison d'Or, tel. 512 17   Public transport
90, ext. 2394

Practical Information

In the street   Inform the nearest police station or the headquarters of the Brussels police, 30 Rue du Marché-au-Charbon (Grand'-Place), tel. 517 96 11

Taxi   Inform the police station nearest to where you engaged the taxi.

Train   If you know the number of the train and its destination inform the nearest station or the terminus.
                       If you do not have the precise details wait a week, and then contact the Leopold Station lost property office, tel. 218 60 50, ext. 6227

Museums

Museums described in   Atomium
Brussels A to Z

Bibliothèque Royale Albert Ier

Chinese Pavilion, see Château Royal de Laeken

Domaine de Gaasbeek

Guild Houses, see Grand'Place

Institut Royal des Sciences Naturelles – Quartier Leopold

Maison Bruegel, see Notre-Dame de la Chapelle

Maison d'Erasme

Maison du Roi (Municipal Museum), see Grand'Place

Manneken-Pis

Manneken-Pis costumes, see Grand'Place, Maison du Roi

Municipal Museum (Maison du Roi), see Grand'Place

Musées Royales des Beaux-Arts de Belgique

Musée du Cinema – Palais des Beaux Arts

Musée de la Dynastie – Palais Royal

Musée de la Gueuze

Musée d'Ixelles – Ixelles

Musée Instrumental

Musée Royal d'Armes et d'Armures, see Porte de Hal

Musée Royal de l'Afrique Centrale

Musée Royal de l'Armée et d'Histoire Militaire, see Palais du Cinquantenaire

Musées Royaux d'Art et d'Histoire, see Palais du Cinquantenaire

Musée Wiertz, see Quartier Leopold

Palais des Académies

Palais des Beaux-Arts

Palais du Cinquantenaire

Porte de Hal

Toones-Museum, see Toones Puppet Theatre

Tour d'Angle (Tour d'Anneessens), see Notre-Dame de la Chapelle

Tour Noire, see Ste-Catherine

Town Hall, see Grand'Place

Waterloo

Archives et Musée de la Vie Viamande (Flemish Museum)   Other Museums
5, Vieux Marché-aux-Grains
Open Mon.–Fri. 1–5 p.m.

Archives Royales (Royal Archives)
2 Rue de Ruysbroek
Open Mon.–Fri. 9–midday and 2–4 p.m.

Bibliotheca Wittockiana (Book-binding Museum)
21–23 Rue du Bemel, Information: tel. 771 85 36

Centre d'Histoire et de Traditions de la Gendarmerie (Police Museum)
98 Rue J. Wytsmans
Open daily 9–midday and 2–5 p.m.

Design Centre
Galerie Ravenstein
Open Mon.–Fri. 10 a.m.–6 p.m.

Musée Camille Lemonnier (home of the writer)
150 Chaussée de Wavre
Open Wed. 1–3 p.m. otherwise by prior arrangement (tel. 512 28 63)

Musée Charlier
Avenue des Arts, St-Josse
Open Sun. 9.30 a.m.–12.30 p.m.

Musée Communal de Woluwé-Saint-Lambert
40 Rue de la Charette
Information: tel. 771 17 23

Musée Communal du Comte de Jette
14 Rue J. Tiebackx
Open Tues.–Fri. 10–midday and 2–4 p.m.

Practical Information

Musée Constantin Meunier
59 Rue de l'Abbaye
Open Mon., Wed., Fri., Sat., 9–midday and 2–5 p.m., Sun.
9.30 a.m.–12.30 p.m.

Musée David and Alice Van Buuren
41 Avenue L. Errera
Open Mon. 2–4 p.m. and by prior arrangement (tel. 344 28 30)

Musée de Chine (Missionary De Scheut's Chinese Museum)
548 Chaussée de Ninove
Open Mon.–Fri. 2.30–5.30 p.m.

Musée de la Banque National (Currency Museum)
9 Rue du Bois Sauvage
Open Mon. 9 a.m.–5 p.m. or by prior arrangement
(tel. 2206–2431)

Musée de la Lunette (Eyeglass Museum)
Rue Royale
Open Mon.–Fri. 9 a.m.–7 p.m.

Musée de la Maison de la Bellone (Bellone House; House of
Actors)
46 Rue de Flandre
Open Mon.–Fri. 10–midday and 2–5 p.m.

Musée de la section d'Histoire et de l'Arts et d'Archéologie de
l'U.L.B. (Collections of the Free University's history, art history
and archaeology faculty)
30 Avenue Antoine Depage
Open Mon.–Thurs. 3–6 p.m.

Musée de la Serrure (Museum of Keys and Locks)
70 Rue des Bouchers
Open Mon.–Sat. 8 a.m.–6 p.m.

Musée de l'Automobile (Automobile Museum)
Under the Place Rogier/Manhattan Center
Information: tel. 219 44 00

Musée de la Résistance (Museum of the Resistance)
14 Rue Van Lint
Information: tel. 523 30 33

Musée de la Radiodiffusion et Télévision Belge (Belgian Radio
and Television Museum)
52 Boulevard Reyers
Information: tel. 737 51 58

Musée de l'Enfant (Museum of Childhood)
32 Rue Tenbosch
Open Wed., Sat., Sun. and public holidays 2.30–5 p.m.

Musée de l'Holographie
30A Rue du Lombard
Open 11 a.m.–7 p.m. daily

Musée de l'Homme (Museum of Mankind)
Metro station Bourse
Open daily 10 a.m.–6 p.m.

Musée de l'Hotel Bellevue (Furniture of the Royal Family)
7 Place des Palais
Open 10 a.m.–4.45 p.m. daily (also guided tours)

Musée de Zoologie et d'Anatomie comparée de l'U.L.B.
(Display of the Free University's zoology and comparative
anatomy collection)
30 Avenue Antoine Depage
Open Mon.–Thurs. 1–4 p.m.

Musée du Chemin de Fer Belge (Belgian Railways Museum)
Gare du Nord (North station)
Open Mon.–Fri. 9 a.m.–5 p.m.

Musée du Costume et de la Dentelle (Museum of Lace and
National Costume)
4–6 Rue de la Violette
Open daily 10–midday and 1–4 p.m.

Musée du Transport Urbain Bruxellois (Brussels Urban
Transport Museum)
364 Avenue de Tervuren
Open Sat., Sun. and public holidays 1–7 p.m.

Musée Géologique et Minéralogique de l'U.L.B. (Free University's geological and mineralogical collections)
30 Avenue Antoine Depage
Open Mon.–Thurs. 9–midday and 2–4 p.m.

Musée Ghysels (Musical Box and Organ Museum)
104 Rue Waelkem
Open daily 3–6 p.m.

Musée Horta
25 Rue Americaine, St-Gilles
Open Tues.–Sun. 2–5.30 p.m.

Musée International de la Presse (Mundaneum)
696 Chaussée de Louvain
Open daily 9–midday and 2–5 p.m.

Musée Michel de Ghelderode
45 Avenue Legrand, Ixelles
Open Mon.–Fri. 10 a.m.–5 p.m.

Musée National de la Figurine Historique (Historical Figurines)
14 Rue J. Tiebackx
Open Tues.–Fri. 10–midday and 2–4 p.m.

Musée Postal (Post and Telecommunications Museum)
40 Place du Grand-Sablon
Open Tues.–Sat. 10 a.m.–4 p.m., Sun. and public holidays
10 a.m.–12.30 p.m.

Musée Privé de la Brasserie
10 Grand'Place
Open daily 10–midday and 2–5 p.m.

Musée Schott
27 Rue du Chêne
closed at present

A room in the Horta Museum

Nightlife

Cabarets	Black Bottom, 1 Rue du Lombard L'Ermitage, 6 Place Sainte-Catherine Le Huchier, 12 Place de Grand Sablon Kartchma, 17 Place du Grand Sablon Le Macao, 1499 Chaussée de Waterloo Le Slave, Rue Scailquin/Place Madou
Jazz clubs	Brussels Jazz Club, 13 Grand'Place Bierodrome, Place Fernand Cocq Les Amies de D.E.S., Rue aux Fleurs
Nightclubs	Au Gaity, 18 Rue Fossé-aux-Loups Moorea, 19 Rue des Dominicains Show Point, 14 Place Stephanie
Dancing	Arlequin, 32a Galerie Louise Bananas, 28 Avenue A. Buyl Circus, 1537 Chaussée de Waterloo Crocodile Club, 5 Rue Duquesnoy Equipe, 40 Rue de Livourne Les Enfants Terribles, 44 Avenue de la Toison d'Or Fanny Horse, 37 Rue de Livourne Happy Few, 19 Avenue Louise
Picturesque bars	Au Bon Vieux Temps, 12 Rue du Marché-aux-Herbes Cirio, 18 Rue de la Bourse Caraquin, 11 Chaussée d'Ixelles

Le Falstaff, 17 Rue Maus
Chez Florio, 20 Rue Marché-aux-Fromages
La Lunette, 3 Place de la Monnaie
Métropole, 31 Place de Brouckére
A la Mort Subite, 17 Rue Montagne-aux-Herbes-Potagères
Le Paon Royal, 6 Rue du Vieux Marché-aux-Grains
Zavel, 7 Place du Grand Sablon

Pets

In view of the stringent regulations regarding the prevention of
rabies you are strongly advised not to attempt to take pets out
of the U.K. or to bring them in when you return.

Postal services

Bruxelles X, Gare du Midi (South Station), 48a Avenue   Post offices
Fonsny: 24-hour service

Centre Monnaie
Gare Centrale (Central Station)
Gare du Nord (North Station)
6 Rue Ducale
17 Rue des Bogards
2 Petite rue des Minimes
9 Boulevard Barthélémy

Brussels letterboxes – highly decorative and bilingual too

Practical Information

Boulevard du Jardin Botanique (Bon Marché)
8 Chaussée de Mons
Bourse
Palais de Justice,
1 Boulevard Charlemagne

Opening times

Open generally from 9 a.m. to 5 p.m.
Closed at week-ends and on public holidays, except for the Avenue de Fonsny post office.

Postal rates

Letters up to 20g (0·7 oz)	Postcards
Domestic 10 Bfr:	Domestic 7.50 Bfr:
Foreign 17 Bfr	Foreign 10 Bfr

The domestic postal rates are also valid for mail to other EEC countries except Britain, Denmark and Ireland. Unlike Belgian currency, Belgian postage stamps cannot be used in Luxembourg.

Public Holidays

1 January (New Year's Day)
Easter Monday
1 May (Labour Day)
Ascension Day (6th Thursday after Easter)
Whit Monday (7th Monday after Easter)
21 July (Belgian National Day)
15 August (Assumption)
1 November (All Saints' Day)
11 November (Armistice Day)
25 December (Christmas Day)
If any of these fall on a Sunday the public holiday will be the following Monday.

Public Transport

Underground (Metro/Pre-metro)

The Brussels underground network currently consists of 42 km (26·25 miles) of metro (underground trains) and pre-metro (partly underground trams). Begun in 1965 the network is due to be extended in the near future. Plans of the underground can be obtained from the Porte de Namur Metro Information Bureau (see also inside the back cover of this guide).
Visitors can get cheap-rate tickets for one day's unlimited travel from the Brussels Tourist Office at 61 Rue du Marché-aux-Herbes (see Tourist Information), or from the railway stations and metro information centres.
Metro stations are marked by a big white M on a blue background.

Bus, tram

Tram-stops and bus-stops have red and white or blue and white signs. Drivers will only stop at the "sur demande" / "op verzoek" (request) stops if you indicate that you want to board the vehicle.

Tickets

On the metro you have to get your ticket punched in the machine at the entrance; on buses and trams these machines are next to the doors at the front.

Inspectors make surprisingly frequent spot-checks and anyone caught travelling without a ticket has to pay a big fine.

Travelling without a ticket

Transfers (transit) from one line to another are free of charge. Tickets to transfer can be obtained by pressing the "transit" button on the machines located at the entrance to the metro or at the front of the trams and buses.

Transfer

The Greater Brussels public transport undertaking has worked out a number of routes under the general title of "Rose des Vents" (compass) so that visitors can make their way by metro, pre-metro, bus and tram to particularly pleasant spots on the outskirts of Brussels.

Rose des Vents routes

Gare Centrale–Heysel–Atomium–Laeken–Gare Centrale

Route Expo "Nord"

De Brouckère–Canal Maritime–Vilvorde–De Brouckère

Route Bruxelles Maritime "Nord-Est"

Gare Centrale–Roodebeek–Woluwé–Tervuren–Gare Centrale

Chemin des Princes "Est"

Gare Centrale–Watermael-Boitsfort–Forêt de Soignes–Gare Centrale

Route Cor de Chasse "Sud-Est"

Gare Centrale–Uccle–Calevoet–Linkebeek–Vieux St-Job–Gare Centrale

Route Monts et Vaux "Sud"

De Brouckère–St-Denis–Forest–Drogenbos–De Brouckère

Route de la Senne "Sud-Ouest"

Gare Centrale–Anderlecht–(Pajottenland)–Gare Centrale

Rue Bruegel et Erasme "Ouest"

Gare Centrale–Groot-Bijgarden–Koekelberg–Berchem–Gare Centrale

Route des Bigards "Nord-Ouest"

S.T.I.B. Information
Metro station Rogier
Metro station Porte de Namur
tel. 511 49 18

Information

T.I.B.
61–63 Rue du Marché-aux Herbes
tel. 513 90 90

Railway stations

Brussels has four international railway stations:

Gare du Nord (North Station), Rue du Progrès, north of the city centre – the main station for eastern destinations.

Gare Centrale (Central Station, i.e. central in location but not in importance), Boulevard de l'Impératrice, near the cathedral in the city centre – some international trains do not stop here!

Gare du Midi (South Station), Boulevard de l'Europe, south-west of the city centre – probably Brussels' busiest station, with trains to France (Paris, Lille) and the North Sea coast (Ostend).

Gare du Quartier Leopold also known as Gare du Luxembourg

Practical Information

(Luxembourg Station), Place du Luxembourg, east of the city centre in the suburb of Ixelles – mainly for commuter services but some international trains from Luxembourg, eastern France (Metz, Strasbourg) and Switzerland (Basle) stop here.

Motorail trains operate from Brussels Schaerbeek.

Information

Information and timetables:
Société Nationale des Chemins de Fer Belges (SNCB), tel. 219 26 40
Time taken by train from Brussels:
– 20 minutes to Leuven and Mechelen (Malines)
– 30 minutes to Antwerp (Anvers/Antwerpen)
– 50 minutes to Namur (Namen)
– 55 minutes to Brugge (Bruges)
– 60 minutes to Tournai (Doornick)
– 65 minutes to Liège (Luik)
– 75 minutes to Ostend (Ostende/Oostende) or the Belgian coast
– 110 minutes to the heart of the Ardennes

Belgium has the world's densest rail network.

Restaurants (Hotel restaurants, see Hotels)

Brussels' many restaurants have long been famous for the excellence and variety of their cuisine. (See Food and drink). Some of the best of them often conceal their proficiency in the culinary arts behind an unassuming façade.

De luxe restaurants

* Bruneau, 73–75 Avenue Broustin
* Comme Chez Soi, 23 Place Rouppe
* Dupont (Claude), 46 Avenue Vital Riethuisen
* Maison du Cygne, 2 Rue Charles Buls
* Villa Lorraine, 75 Avenue du Vivier d'Oie
Barbizon, 95 Welriekende Dreef, B-1900 Jezuz-Eik (Overijse)
Berkenhof, 5 Valkeniersdreef, B-2850 Keerbergen
Ecailler du Palais Royal, 18–20 Rue Bodenbroek
Kolmer, 18 Drève de Carloo
Michel, 31 Gossetlaan, B-1720 Groot-Bijgarden
L'Oasis, 9 Place Marie-José

Other restaurants

Aloyse Kloos, 2 Terhulpsteenweg, B-1990 Hoeilaart
L'Ami Michel, 17 Place du Samedi
Les Arcades, 1441 Chaussée de Waterloo
Aux Armes de Bruxelles, 13 Rue des Bouchers
Auberge de Boendael, 12 Square du Vieux Tilleul
Le Béarnais, 318 Boulevard L. Mettewie
Bernard, 93 Rue de Namur
De Bijgarden, 20 Rue Isidoor, B-1720 Groot-Bijgarden
Le Chalet Rose, 49 Avenue du Bois de Cambre
Le Cheval Blanc, 204 Rue Haute
Chez Christopher, 5 Place de la Chapelle
Chez Jean, 6 Rue des Chapeliers
De Reu (Roland), 226–228 Chaussée de Bruxelles
Les Délices de la Mer, 1020 Chaussée de Waterloo
Au Duc d'Ahrenberg, 9 Place du Petit Sablon

Brussels restaurants combine elegance with comfort

Jacques, 44 Quai aux Briques
Grand Café, 76 Boulevard Anspach
Ferme Madeleine, 20 Rue de la Montagne
Maison du Seigneur, 389 Chaussée de Tervuren, B-1410
Waterloo
Le Marmiton, 43a Rue des Bouchers
Mon Manège à Toi, 1 Rue Neerveld
Ogenblik, 1 Galerie des Princes
Le Piano à Bretelles, 40 Rue A. De Witte
La Pomme Cannelle, 6 Avenue F. D. Roosevelt
Saint-Jean des Prés, 5–7 Quai au Bois à Brûler
Scheltema, 7 Rue des Dominicains
La Sirène d'Or, 1a Place Sainte-Catherine
Taverne du Passage, 30 Galerie de la Reine
Trente Rue de la Paille, 30 Rue de la Paille
De Ultieme Hallucinatie, 316 Rue Royale

Fleur de Jasmin, 138 Rue Bemel   Chinese
La Fontaine de Jade, 5 Avenue de Tervuren
Ming's Garden, 11 Rue du Grand Cerf
Pavillon Imperial, 1296 Chaussée de Waterloo
Au Thé de Pékin, 16 Rue de la Vierge Noire

Maharaja, 72 Quai aux Briques   Indian

Le Cambodge, 77 Rue Washington   Cambodian

Al Piccolo Mondo, 21–23 Rue Jourdan   Italian
Osteria del Barone, 26 Rue de Flandre
Le Canard Sauvage, 194 Chaussée de la Hulpe

137

Japanese	Samourai, 28 Rue Fossé-aux-Loups
Creole	La Martinique, Avenue Général Eisenhower
Mongolian	La Maison d'Attila, 36–38 Avenue du Prince de Ligne.
Thai	L'Eléphant Bleu, 1120 Chaussée de Waterloo La Thailande, 29 Avenue Legrand
Vietnamese	Les Baguettes Imperiales, 70 Avenue J. Sobieski La Tour d'Asie, 154 Boulevard A. Reyers
Vegetarian	Le Paradoxe, 329 Chaussée d'Ixelles Tsampa, 109 Rue de Livourne

Shopping

Brussels as a metropolis has also become an important shopping centre in recent years and shopping has come to be focused on two areas known as uptown and downtown.

Uptown

Uptown around the Place Louise, Avenue Louise, Avenue de la Toison d'Or, Boulevard de Waterloo and Porte de Namur and the galleries leading off them is where you find the exclusive expensive establishments, the famous fashion houses and other well-known names.
A stroll along the Chaussee d'Ixelles and its side streets is less sumptuous but just as pleasant.

Rue Neuve, one of the city's busiest pedestrian precincts

The main shopping street downtown is the Rue Neuve pedestrian precinct with its department stores, specialist shops and the two complexes – Inno and City 2.

Downtown

There are also plenty of good shops on Boulevard Adolphe Max, Place de Brouckère and Place de la Monnaie as well as on Boulevard Anspach.

Jewellers, fashion boutiques and elegant leather shops are to be found in the narrow Rue des Fripiers and in the Rue au Beurre or the Petite Rue au Beurre.

A speciality of Brussels is its galleries and shopping arcades, the most famous probably being the Galeries Saint-Hubert, although the Galerie Bortier, Galerie Agora, Galerie du Centre and Passage 44 also deserve a mention.

The Woluwé Shopping Centre in Woluwé-St-Lambert and Westland Shopping Centre in Anderlecht are currently the biggest of their kind in Europe.

Outskirts

Good buys in Brussels are confectionery, chocolates (excellent pralines) speculoos (gingerbread), Brussels lace, crystal, pewter, weapons and jewellery.

Souvenirs

Exquisite hand-made lace can be found on the Grand'Place, in the Galeries Saint-Hubert the Rue de l'Etuve and the Rue de la Regence.

Lace

The history of Brussels is closely linked to the history of the art of tapestry-making, of weaving together woollen, silken, gold and silver threads with the skill of an artist.

Tapestries

Genuine old masterpieces can be duly admired in Brussels'

A sample of Brussels' world-famous tapestries

museums (see entry) and outlying castles. Modern tapestries are for sale in the Rue des Ailes and on the Boulevard de Waterloo.

See A to Z, Boulevards
See A to Z, Rue Neuve

Sport

Big stadiums	Stade Emile Verse (S.C. Anderlecht) Avenue Th. Verbeek
	Stade du Heysel 135 Avenue du Marathon
	Stade de l'Université Libre 22 Avenue Paul Heger
	Stade Edmond Machtens 61 Rue Charles Malis
	Stade Fallon Woluwé-St-Lambert
	Stade Joseph Marien 233 Chaussée de Bruxelles
Racecourses	Boitsfort 51 Chaussée de la Hulpe
	Sterrebeek Avenue du Roy de Blicky
	Groenendael Avenue Leopold II
Swimming-pools	Calypso 60 Avenue Leopold Wiener
	Poseidon 2 Avenue des Vaillants
	Complexe Sportif d'Etterbeek 69 Rue des Champs
	Bains de Bruxelles 28 Rue de Chevreuil
	Bains de Forest 34 Rue Berthelot
	Bains de Ganshoren 10 Place Fabiola
	Bains d'Ixelles Rue de la Natation
	Bains L. Nameche 93 Rue Van Kalek

Bains de St-Gilles
38 Rue de la Perche

Bains de St-Josse
23 Rue St-Francois

Bains de Schaerbeek
54 Rue de Jerusalem

Solarium du Centenaire   Open-air pools
Avenue de Meisse

Solarium d'Evere
121 Rue de Genève

Solarium du Centre Sportif de Woluwé-St-Pierre
2 Avenue Salome

Piscine Longchamps
46 Avenue Defré

Patinoire à Glace Forest National   Ice-rinks
36 Avenue du Globe

Patinoire à Glace Poseidon
2 Avenue des Vaillants

Bois de la Cambre   Jogging
Forêt de Soignes
Parc de Tervuren

Riding and tennis, as well as hockey, rugby and roller-skating,   Other sports
are very popular in Brussels.

Taxis (Cabs)

Taxis Bleus S.A., tel. 268 10 10   Taxi firms (selection)
Taxi Jaunes S.A., tel. 647 99 30
Taxi-Radio Bruxellois S.A., tel. 513 33 55
Taxis Unifiés, tel. 640 40 40
Taxis Verts, tel. 347 47 47

Telephone/Telegrams

Call-charges are displayed in the telephone kiosks. Make sure
you have enough 5-franc pieces.
Telephone kiosks, from which international calls can be made
and telegrams can be sent, bear the name of the countries
concerned.
Brussels has a 24-hour "Help Line" giving general advice in
English: tel. 648 40 14

Gare du Midi (South Station), 1d Avenue Fonsny   Telephone/telegraph offices
Open Mon.–Fri. 9 a.m.–5.15 p.m., Sat. 8 a.m.–4 p.m.   (R.T.T.)

Practical Information

17 Boulevard de L'Impératrice
Open daily 8 a.m.–10 p.m.

23a Rue de Brabant
Open Mon.–Fri. 9 a.m.–5.15 p.m.

Place du Luxembourg
Open Mon.–Fri. 9–midday, 12.30–5.15 p.m.

Brussels National Airport
Open daily 7 a.m.– 10 p.m.

Theatres and Concert Halls

Booking

Seats for theatres and concerts can be booked by telephone using TELETIB, the convenient service provided by the Brussels Tourist Office. Tickets for shows and events can also be obtained from the Tourist Office in the Rue du Marché-aux-Herbes (see Tourist Information).
Most theatres and concert halls have their own box offices.

Information

tel. 513 83 28/29, 513 89 40

Theatres and concert halls

L'Atelier
51 Rue du Commerce, tel. 511 20 65

Atelier Sainte-Anne
20 Rue Sainte-Anne, tel. 513 19 28

Auditorium 44
44 Passage, Boulevard du Jardin Botanique, tel. 219 55 31

Palais des Beaux-Arts
23 Rue Ravenstein, tel. 218 27 35

Beursshouwburg
22 Rue Auguste Orts, tel. 511 25 25

Centre culturel d'Auderghem
185 Boulevard du Souverain, tel. 660 03 03

Centre culturel et artistique d'Uccle
47 Rue Rouge, tel. 374 64 84

Cirque Royal
81 Rue de l'Enseignement, tel. 218 20 15, 219 51 49

Compagnie Claude Volter
98 Avenue Fr. Legrain, tel. 762 09 63

Conservatoire Royal de musique
30 Rue de la Regence, tel. 511 44 95

Koninklijke Vlaamse Shouwburg
146 Rue de Laeken, tel. 219 49 44

Maison de la Culture de Woluwé-St-Pierre
93 Avenue Thielemans, tel. 771 14 93

Opéra National – Théâtre Royal de la Monnaie
Place de la Monnaie, tel. 218 12 01/02

Théâtre 140
140 Avenue E. Plasky, tel. 734 44 31, 734 46 31

Théâtre de l'Esprit Frappeur
28 Rue Josaphat, tel. 217 06 69

Théâtre de l'Ile Saint-Louis
5 Rue des Esperonniers, tel. 513 24 93

Théâtre de Poche
Bois de la Cambre, Châlet du Gymnase, tel. 649 17 27

Théâtre Molière
6 Galerie des Princes, tel. 513 58 00

Théâtre National Centre International Rogier
Place Rogier, tel. 217 03 03

Théâtre Poème
30 Rue d'Ecosse, tel. 538 63 57/58

Théâtre Royal des Galeries
32 Galeries du Roi, tel. 512 04 07, 513 39 60

Théâtre Royal du Parc
3 Rue de la Loi, tel. 512 23 39, 512 48 23

Toone VII
See A to Z, Toones Puppet Theatre

Raffinerie du Plank
21 Rue de Manchester, tel. 523 18 34

Beursschouwburg (Flemish)
22 Rue A. Orts, tel. 511 25 25

Puppet theatres and
children's theatre

B.K.T. (Flemish)
12 Rue de la Chaufferette, Brussels, tel. 511 86 09

Brialmont Theatre (Flemish)
11 Rue Brialmont, Brussels, tel. 217 24 21

Centre Culturel de Béco
116 Avenue E. de Beco, Ixelles, tel. 735 03 21

Théâtre des Jeunes de la Ville de Bruxelles
57 Rue du Marais, Brussels, tel. 217 57 54

Théâtre du Ratinet
Ferme Rose, 44 Avenue De Fré, Uccle, tel. 375 15 63

Théâtre de la Vie
100 Avenue du Haras, Woluwé-Saint-Pierre, tel. 762 34 29

Time

In the winter Belgium observes Central European Time (1 hour ahead of Greenwich Mean Time) then switches to summer time (2 hours ahead of GMT) from the end of March until the end of September.

Tipping

Cinema and theatre	Usherettes expect to be tipped (about 10 Bfr).
Hotels	Service is included.
Restaurants	16 per cent service and 19 per cent VAT are included but it is customary to round up the bill.
Hairdresser	If service is not included in the price, the tip should be about 20 per cent of the total.
Taxi	The tip is included in the fare.
Public toilets	If there is no charge the tip should be 5 to 10 Bfr.
Porter	Porters at the airport want 20 Bfr per piece of luggage on weekdays and otherwise at least 25 Bfr. Porters at Brussels' stations want 20 Bfr per piece of luggage during the day and 25 Bfr at night.

Tourist Information

Tourisme Information Bruxelles

Brussels Tourist Information Office is located at:
61 Rue du Marché-aux-Herbes, 1000 Brussels
tel. 513 90 90, 513 89 40, telex: B.BRU.B. 63 245
Adjacent to the Grand'Place, it is jointly managed by the General Commissariat for Tourism, the Tourist Board for the Province of Brabant and T.I.B., Tourisme Information Bruxelles.

Reception service:
There is a reception service on the ground floor, with multilingual hostesses who can supply information about Brussels, Brabant and the rest of Belgium.
This service is available to the public daily in winter from 9 a.m. to 6 p.m. including Sundays and public holidays, and, in summer from 9 a.m. to 8 p.m. (7 p.m. at week-ends).
The hostesses can also be contacted by telephoning 512 30 30 and via the Information Offices at the Gare du Midi and Gare du Nord (see Railway stations) and at the Rogier metro station. They can make hotel reservations and obtain tickets for cultural events. This can also be done by telephone using the TELETIB system.
Other special services include the Brussels Official Guide, special tourist tickets for the city's public transport (see entry), advice on car-hire (see Car hire), cassette-hire for taped guided tours of the Grand'Place, etc.

Brussels Tourist Information Office (T.I.B.) also keeps the
Calendar of events (see entry), up to date in terms of cultural
events and tourism.

Bruxelles-Congrès:
The special conference department helps with the preparation
and organisation of international conferences in Brussels (see
Conference information) and the T.I.B. provides multilingual
hostesss for fairs, exhibitions and conferences.
Guided tours in Brussels and Brabant:
The T.I.B. office is also the secretariat for guided tours in
Brussels and Brabant.
Its information service "S.V.P" can be reached on 513 89 40.

There is a visitor information centre (see Airport) in the
baggage claim area 722 30 00/01.

Airport

Acotra
38 Rue de la Montagne, Brussels, tel. 513 44 80, 513 44 89.
This association for foreign students also has an information
point at the airport, tel. 751 07 09.

Reception of young people

Infor-J
27 Rue du Marché-aux-Herbes, Brussels, tel. 512 32 74
Open Mon.–Fri. 10 a.m.–7 p.m., Sat. midday–7 p.m.
There is also a reception service available in the summer at the
Gare du Midi (South Station) tel. 522 58 66.

SOS-Youth
27 Rue de la Blanchisserie, Brussels, tel. 736 36 36.
A 24-hour service for young people in need of counselling.

Travel Documents

A passport or identity card is needed to enter Belgium and for
a stay of more than 3 months visitors from outside the EEC
require a visa.

Passport/identity card

Driving licence and car registration papers from EEC countries
are accepted. A Green Card is required for non-EEC visitors. All
foreign cars must display an approved national identity plate.

Driving licence/car
registration papers

Boats over 5·5 m (18 ft) long being brought into Belgium by
road, etc. must have a triptych (customs' certificate) or Carnet
de Passage (customs' certificate for several countries).

Boat papers

Weather forecast and road conditions

Tel. 991
This is the number to call for a regularly up-dated weather
forecast and, from November to March, information on road
conditions.
Reports on winter road conditions can also be had from:

Royal Automobile Club de Belgique,
tel. 230 08 68 (24-hour service)

Touring Club de Belgique,
tel. 233 22 11, 7 a.m.–8 p.m.

Information line, tel. 230 57 75

Gendarmerie, tel. 749 00 00, ext. 2101
weekdays 6.30 a.m.–7 p.m.

When to visit Brussels

The best time to visit Belgium is in the spring and summer, i.e.
from May to September. Autumn is often windy and rainy
although this time of year also has its attractions because of the
many folk festivals, etc.

Youth Hostels (selection)

*Auberge Bruegel
2 Rue du Saint-Esprit, Brussels, tel. 511 04 36

Centre international des Etudiants
26 Rue de Parme, St-Gilles, tel. 537 89 61

Foyer protestant "David Livingstone"
119 Avenue Coghen, Uccle, tel. 343 30 89
(young men only)

Louvain en Woluwé
53 Jardin Martin V, Woluwé-St-Lambert, tel. 770 99 51

Maison internationale des Etudiants
205 Chaussée de Wavre, Etterbeek, tel. 648 85 29
(students only)

Sleep-Well Auberge du Marais
27 Rue de la Blanchisserie, Brussels, tel. 218 50 50

Vrij Universiteit van Brussel
1 Boulevard du Triomphe, Etterbeek, tel. 641 88 31

◀ *Floral carpet in the Grand'Place*

Useful Telephone Numbers at a Glance

Airlines
- Air Canada   513 62 10
- British Airways   219 42 20
- Pan Am   751 81 95
- Qantas   513 27 92
- SABENA   511 90 30
- South African Airways   218 48 00
- TWA   513 79 15

Embassies
- Australia   511 39 97
- Canada   513 79 40
- Eire   513 66 33
- New Zealand   512 10 40
- South Africa   230 68 45
- United Kingdom   217 90 00
- United States of America   513 38 30

Emergency calls
- Ambulance   900
- RACB breakdown service in Brussels   736 59 59
- Touring Secours break-down service   233 22 11
- Traffic police   901

Information
- Belgian railways in London   01–734 1491
- Flight information   751 81 60
  SABENA   511 42 20
- Motoring organisations
  Royal Automobile Club de Belgique (RACB), Ixelles   230 08 10
  Touring Club Royal de Belgique (TCB)   233 22 11
  Tourist guides Brussels and Brabant   513 89 40
- Tourist information offices in Brussels (tourism centre) 513 90 90, 513 89 40
  at Brussels Airport   720 91 41
  in London   01–499 5379
  in New York   758 81 30
- Train times in Brussels   219 26 40
- Weather forecast   991
- Young people's reception
  Acotra   513 44 80, 513 44 89
  Infor-J   512 32 74
  SOS-youth   736 36 36

Lost property offices
- Airport   511 18 60
- Police   513 28 40
- Public transport   512 17 90 ext. 2334
- SABENA   720 91 13
- Train   219 26 40

Telephone dialling codes
- to Brussels from the United Kingdom   010 32 2
- from Brussels to
  Australia   00 61
  Canada   00 1
  United Kingdom   00 44
  United States of America   00 1

Notes

Plan of the Brussels Underground

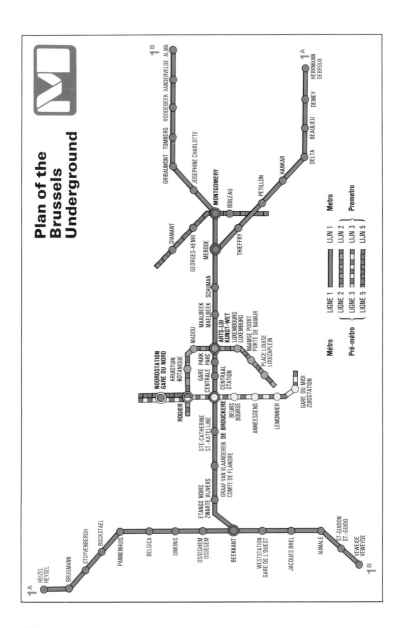

Baedeker's Travel Guides

"The maps and illustrations are lavish. The arrangement of information (alphaebetically by city) makes it easy to use the book."

—*San Francisco Examiner-Chronicle*

What's there to do and see in foreign countries? Travelers who rely on Baedeker, one of the oldest names in travel literature, will miss nothing. Baedeker's bright red, internationally recognized covers open up to reveal fascinating A-Z directories of cities, towns, and regions, complete with their sights, museums, monuments, cathedrals, castles, gardens and ancestral homes—an approach that gives the traveler a quick and easy way to plan a vacation itinerary.

And Baedekers are filled with over 200 full-color photos and detailed maps, including a full-size, fold-out roadmap for easy vacation driving. Baedeker—the premier name in travel for over 140 years.

Please send me the books checked below and fill in order form on reverse side.

☐ **Austria** $14.95
0-13-056127-4
☐ **Caribbean** $14.95
0-13-056143-6
☐ **Egypt** $15.95
0-13-056358-7
☐ **France** $14.95
0-13-055814-1
☐ **Germany** $14.95
0-13-055830-3
☐ **Great Britain** $14.95
0-13-055855-9
☐ **Greece** $14.95
0-13-056002-2
☐ **Israel** $14.95
0-13-056176-2
☐ **Italy** $14.95
0-13-055897-4
☐ **Japan** $15.95
0-13-056382-X
☐ **Loire** $9.95
0-13-056375-7

☐ **Mediterranean Islands** $14.95
0-13-056862-7
☐ **Mexico** $14.95
0-13-056069-3
☐ **Netherlands, Belgium, and Luxembourg** $14.95
0-13-056028-6
☐ **Portugal** $14.95
0-13-056135-5
☐ **Provence/Cote d'Azur** $9.95
0-13-056938-0
☐ **Rhine** $9.95
0-13-056466-4
☐ **Scandinavia** $14.95
0-13-056085-5
☐ **Spain** $14.95
0-13-055913-X
☐ **Switzerland** $14.95
0-13-056044-8
☐ **Tuscany** $9.95
0-13-056482-6
☐ **Yugoslavia** $14.95
0-13-056184-3

Please turn the page for an order form and a list of additional Baedeker Guides.

A series of city guides filled with colour photographs and detailed maps and floor plans from one of the oldest names in travel publishing:

Please send me the books checked below:

☐ **Amsterdam** $10.95 0-13-057969-6		☐ **Madrid** $10.95 0-13-058033-3	
☐ **Athens** $10.95 0-13-057977-7		☐ **Moscow** $10.95 0-13-058041-4	
☐ **Bangkok** $10.95 0-13-057985-8		☐ **Munich** $10.95 0-13-370370-3	
☐ **Berlin** $10.95 0-13-367996-9		☐ **New York** $10.95 0-13-058058-9	
☐ **Brussels** $10.95 0-13-368788-0		☐ **Paris** $10.95 0-13-058066-X	
☐ **Copenhagen** $10.95 0-13-057993-9		☐ **Rome** $10.95 0-13-058074-0	
☐ **Florence** $10.95 0-13-369505-0		☐ **San Francisco** $10.95 0-13-058082-1	
☐ **Frankfurt** $10.95 0-13-369570-0		☐ **Singapore** $10.95 0-13-058090-2	
☐ **Hamburg** $10.95 0-13-369687-1		☐ **Tokyo** $10.95 0-13-058108-9	
☐ **Hong Kong** $10.95 0-13-058009-0		☐ **Venice** $10.95 0-13-058116-X	
☐ **Jerusalem** $10.95 0-13-058017-1		☐ **Vienna** $10.95 0-13-371303-2	
☐ **London** $10.95 0-13-058025-2			

PRENTICE HALL PRESS

Order Department—Travel Books

200 Old Tappan Road

Old Tappan, New Jersey 07675

In U.S. include $1 postage and handling for 1st book, 25¢ each additional book. Outside U.S. $2 and 50¢ respectively.

Enclosed is my check or money order for $_____

NAME_____

ADDRESS_____

CITY_____STATE_____ZIP_____